"As a young woman in finance, I found this book to be extremely empowering. Dr. Virginia is an inspiring individual whose resilience and determination to pave the way for women like me is incredible. We truly stand on the shoulders of giants."

– **Ellen Long**, MBA, Wealth Advisor,
Long Family Office, COO, Long Business Advisors

"Dr. Virginia has given readers the opportunity to share in both her successes and struggles, paving the way for women in generations after her to fight for a seat at the table. She did this throughout her life as a wife, mother, and pioneer in a male-dominated industry. Her journey fully supports the truth that success isn't a straight line, but the struggles make the successes that much sweeter."

– **Nicole Peterkin**, Author, *If You Love Your Family Save Like It*, and Owner/Financial Advisor at Peterkin Financial, LLC

"*A First Lady of Finance* highlights the importance of commitment and determination in business and in life. This book was also impactful because it helped me look at life in the bigger picture, giving me more clarity with respect to the test of time and the purpose of my life. Though specifically geared towards women, I recommend this book for anyone – man or woman, young or old."

– **Glenn Davis**, Jr., Financial Strategist,
and Author, *Mission: True Freedom*

A
FIRST LADY
of FINANCE

A
First Lady
of Finance

Dr. Virginia Lee McKemie-Belt

NEXT CENTURY
PUBLISHING

A First Lady Of Finance
Pioneering The Way For Women Today

Published by Next Century Publishing
Las Vegas, Nevada
www.NextCenturyPublishing.com

ISBN: 978-1-68102-078-5
Library of Congress Control Number: 2015950251

Printed in the United States of America

ACKNOWLEDGMENTS

My granddaughter, Michele (Mimi) Wager, receives my special regard for her insightful comments, which brings the past into the present at the beginning of almost every chapter. Michele wrote the Forward and the Postscript (1) and carefully enclosed these memoirs in her own interruption of my life.

Doris Falck and Kit McGee who read and re-read all of the chapters and made valuable comments.

Shawn Raymor who manned the computer and kept me connected to the modern age of computer generated books.

Simon Presland, our editor, whose suggestions and encouragement were invaluable.

Long Y. Liu provided updated proofs and his superb computer skills to my enterprise.

Special thanks to my daughter, Patricia McGill, who spent her vacation proofing this book of my memoirs.

Dedicated to
My husband, Dr. J. R. Belt, who tolerated
and even assisted me in my journey through the glass ceiling.

TABLE OF CONTENTS

A
First Lady
of Finance

FOREWORD

While the Master of Ceremonies, standing on her left, was enumerating and praising her credentials, the business man on her right whispered, "If you were my wife, you would be home where you belong, having babies."

Before she could formulate a reply, the MC said, "Now I give you Dr. McKemie-Belt, our very talented speaker."

During her speech, she analyzed some anti-business legislation for about twenty-five minutes and ended with these words, "A speech is like a love affair; it is easy to start, but hard to end, so I will just say thank you for listening." After accepting complements, comments, and questions for about ten minutes, she turned to do battle with the "macho" male on her right, but his seat was empty.

That lady was my grandmother, Dr. Virginia Lee McKemie-Belt. Nana, as we call her, reminded me that this incident happened over half a century ago, but it is a good example of a male response when confronted by a lady making her mark in the men-only field of business, finance, and investments. She was a true modern-day pioneer, following her dreams as she maneuvered the mine-fields of the male dominated financial arena. She began this journey more than fifty years ago. A few doors were closed to her, but many more were pried open by her. Throughout her journey, she encountered gender discrimination and gender embarrassment, but in the end encountered gender rewards.

This is the extraordinary story of Nana's trials and victories throughout her life, from a small farm in southern Illinois to the very top of her chosen profession, where she was listed by *Who's Who* as one of the "One Thousand Women of the World" alongside Queen Elizabeth I and II, Madam Curie and Cleopatra.

During her journey she garnered many firsts, including:

- First lady faculty member in the School of Business at CSU

- First lady professor to be featured on the *This Is Your Life* television show, hosted by Ralph Edwards

- First and only spokeswoman to represent the American Bankers Association at the Asiatic Currency Unit in Singapore

- First lady professor to be bounced from the Exchange Club in NY, only to be readmitted via the freight elevator, as she was the scheduled speaker for the day

- The only lady among twenty educators from all over the United States to be the guest of the Chinese government for six weeks

As my grandmother made her way through the world of finance, she took many jobs such as teaching math, dramatics director, college professor of economics history, inventory analyst, and trip coordinator. My grandfather, Dr. J.R. Belt, was an educational administrator, thus they had to mesh two careers.

Often, as one accepted a new position, the other had to move and look for a new job.

A high point in her journey occurred in 2005 when she was introduced as the woman who broke the gender code for women business students before a black-tie crowd of graduating honorees and notable alumni in corporate America. When introducing my grandmother, the M.C. (Master of Ceremonies) stated, "She broke the glass ceiling for women in Business Education and she did it with dignity and with calm effectiveness." This introduction was especially appropriate since many of the honor graduates were women. However, the older alumni notables were all men! How times have changed.

When my grandmother finally decided to listen to the many people who urged her to publish her life's story, she recruited me. My first job was to sort through the many boxes of taped and typed chapters, newspaper and magazine articles, and the countless letters, programs and commendations, and place them into some kind of timeline. The most difficult part of my job was to decide what to include. Given Nana's inspiring life it was hard to leave any details out. Nana and I decided to format her story as an autobiography written by her within a biography written by me. She weaves the events of her life around the economy so skillfully that the reader gains an enhanced knowledge of the economic history of the 20th century without realizing he or she is being taught.

A few years ago, the Enhancement (motivational) Club sponsored a program called the *Human Side of the Super Achiever*, and my grandmother was invited as a speaker. Within five minutes, she had the entire audience in awe and laughter as she related many of the same stories she included in this book. Some of these stories include the fate of twenty-four chickens, a drunken cat, exploding beer bottles, a trip up the freight elevator, and the Peach Formal episodes. When she mentioned the five cent triple dip ice cream cones, WWII food and gas ration cards, and bailouts, heads began to nod and some in the audience seemed to say "I remember when . . ."

I invite you to sit back in your favorite chair and enjoy the story of Nana's life.

CHAPTER 1

What creates a person like my Grandmother? Social scientists have debated the effects of heredity versus environment on personality development for ages. Is it genes or geography, or perhaps a combination of both?

Today, more and more people are studying genealogy to discover who they are and how they got that way. My sister, Melinda, and I have urged Nana to tell us about our heredity to better understand how it might possibly affect us and our children. Nana provided the information that we requested in a series of audio tapes. As I listened to some of the stories and experiences she related, I found them fascinating and I trust that you will too. These are Nana's words to us.

In the Beginning

Michele and Melinda, you have asked me to relate what I know about your ancestors. I admit that much of what I tell you comes from hearsay, without any substantive proof. With that caveat, let me tell you what I have heard or learned from investigation.

Your grandfather, James Radford Belt, Papa, as you called him, and I took a trip to Ireland in search of his ancestors. We believe that his last name was originally "0"Belt. They seem to have been belt makers, and were concentrated in the southwest part of Ireland near Dingle Bay. In those days, it was customary to take a last name from your profession. However, we could find no direct line. They might have migrated to the United States during the Great Potato Famine. There is a town in

Maryland called Beltsville, located northeast of Washington, D.C. We had hoped to travel there some day to look up a number of "Belts" we found in the telephone directory.

The Irish are very brave, but quick and loud in the defense of their beliefs. Your great-grandfather, Charlie Belt, said Papa could be heard all over the town of Shawneetown arguing about his "rights." As the youngest of four boys, he learned to fight and tried to win by being loudest.

We know very little about his mother. His parents were divorced when he was four. Papa was reared by a stepmother who provided all of life's necessitates, but very little love or affection. All Papa seemed to know about his mother was that she was deeply religious and spent most of her time in church or on her knees. The eldest son, Doc Belt, tried to improve her economic condition but she gave away almost everything that was given to her.

On my side, the McKemies were my father's family, and the Loucks were my mother's kinfolk. Fortunately, there has been much more study done on the McKemies. In fact, while in Scotland, we found the tartan of the McKemies. I bought a five-piece outfit in that beautiful green and red design.

But I must say I have some doubts about the tartan because I saw it in another store labeled "The McKinsey Clan." The first trace we have is a young Scot landing in Georgia. We believe that he must have run afoul of the British or he was a second son who came to the New World to seek his fortune. The next trace we have of them was in Tennessee. There are some books and pamphlets featuring the McKemees or McKamie.

At the Genealogical Hall in Salt Lake City, Utah, I ran across a book about a Susan McKemie. She was a real pioneer, and I believe she was your ancestor; there has been a Susan McKemie in every generation. She was independent, tough, and was a "Medicine Woman." She had no formal education, but understood herbs and Indian medication. She rode a horse to make house-calls.

The rest of the story is more verifiable. About 175 years ago two brothers, Tom and Charlie McKemie came to Southern Illinois, divided the land

and started a little town called Benton. It is reported by Old Timers that your great-grandfather, Tom, rode a big white charger stallion through town, and used his whip literally and liberally on anyone who impeded his progress.

Grandfather was indeed a Scottish Laird. There was a room in their big house on the hill that was called the Throne Room. We grandchildren lived in fear of being called to the Throne Room for a "dressing down."

Your great great-grandmother Monneyham was a tiny thing who bore eight boys including your great-grandfather, Charles Franklin McKemie, and three daughters. She was fiercely southern and would say to me, "Virginia Lee, mark my words, the South will rise again and "whoop" those dam-m-m-n Yankees." She was also responsible for naming me, Virginia Lee, after her hero, Robert E. Lee. Around her, everyone had to use my full name, Virginia Lee, or they might be hit by her ever-ready broom.

Your great great-grandmother and her growing daughters and younger sons (who had to fetch food from the gardens or storehouses) prepared two big meals each day for about twenty-five or more members of the family and the hired help. After the noon meal, or dinner as we called it, everything uneaten was covered with a white cloth and you were on your own for supper, scrounging through the leftovers. Afternoons were hers to mend, read her Bible, or receive guests.

The Loucks Heritage: Your great-grandfather was of German descent.

His father was a fur trader and married an Indian maiden. My mother came from that lineage. One day I heard my grandmother and her sister, Aunt Ida, mention something about Indian heritage. When I asked them about it, they said I had misheard. It wasn't "cool" to be Indian back then. I wish I had investigated further; we might be descended from one of the very rich tribes that run casinos today.

Their house had a big wrap around porch, and a big flower garden between the house and the country lane. My grandmother was justifiably proud of her garden, and was asked to decorate their village church every Sunday, even using dried flowers in the wintertime. They cultivated all kinds of berries, grapes, fruit trees and nut bushes. Sundays were like a "smorgasbord" of all things good.

In summary, it appears that your ancestors carried "good genes," were industrious, and lived in a challenging environment that made them strong.

CHAPTER 2

"Rain, rain go away" and then as an afterthought, a plea, "Please come again another day." It has been raining 24/7 for over a week with the velocity and volume common to the Puget Sound area of western Washington, but the number of days of unrelenting down pour is uncommon. It makes newcomers like us wonder why we had left the semi-arid states of Nevada, Arizona, New Mexico or California. Even the natives are beginning to wonder when or if it is going to stop. One grizzled old timer was heard to grumble, "Begorra God, this is a bit much."

Even though the inclement weather has confined me to the house, it allows me to get on with my labor of love—telling Nana's story.

Virginia Lee McKemie was born from the union of Charles Franklin McKemie and Bessie Nova Loucks. The two families lived within ten miles of each other, near the town of Benton, Illinois. From the stories Nana told us, she spent time with these close-knit families on alternating Sundays. During those formative years . . . but let's allow her to tell you how it all happened.

Growing up in the Great Depression

I was born in 1923 at home. Years later, someone gave me a pamphlet called "Pages of Time – 1923." Some of the headlines read: "Rare Treasures Found In Tut's Tomb"; "Nazi Party Holds First Congress In Munich"; "First Sound On Film Movie Shown"; "Teapot Dome Scandal Breaks." One page showed some 1923 prices: New Car: $295.00, New

House: $7,400.00, Loaf of Bread: 9 cents, Gallon of Gas: 12 cents, Dow Jones Average: 94, Gold per Ounce: $20.00. To put these in perspective, the average wage was only $2,126.00 per year!

I don't know if I remembered this, or if it was repeated so often that I thought I did. One Sunday we were all seated around the big twenty-five-seat table, and Grandfather McKemie pointed to me and said, "I charge you all to see that she goes all the way to her doctorate. It would be nice if she became the first lady PhD in the county. In spite of her youth, I'm surprised at her grasp of business ideas. Steer her that way." It was as if Grandfather McKemie was predicting my destiny. That meant watching over my school grades. In the 7th grade, I was having trouble with art and music. Grandfather ordered a violin, a set of oil paints and teachers to solve that problem. I took to the oil paints and was soon painting scenes, which I copied off calendars that became a favorite gift of my family. I believe half the homes in Benton had one of my pictures. But the violin was a complete disaster! I finally learned to play "Twinkle, Twinkle, Little Star." Mom and Dad banished me from their earshot, so I'd go up on a knoll to practice, but that was within Grandfather's earshot. He couldn't stand the noise either so he ordered a piano and a new teacher. That worked better, but I still play very mechanically.

My aunts and uncles never let me forget Grandfather's charge to everyone. In fact, years later when my engagement was announced, an uncle wrote from Africa, where he was stationed, and said, "If you won't get married and have forty-eleven kids, I'll take you to Europe when I get home."

When I was six, a little sister, Donna, came to be my playmate. We spent many a happy hour during the long summers playing games we would make up. One of our favorites was playing the royal family of England. I was Princess Elizabeth and Donna played Princess Margaret. We wore crowns of clover heads and lace curtains as robes.

We had a pleasant, but financially restrained childhood. This was the time of the Great Depression of the 1930s. We were never hungry because the farm furnished most of our needs. In the morning Dad would get the wood cook stove going, then he would fry steaks, pork chops, sausage, bacon or rabbit, along with, eggs, eggs, and more eggs! With the oven hot, Mom would bake pies, cakes and biscuits. Once in Jr. High, I asked if we could have "light bread." What I wouldn't give for her biscuits or slices of chocolate pie now!

Dad worked three jobs. He worked at the mines, mowing the highway, and on the farm. At about 4:00 p.m. we would wait with bated breathes for the mine whistle. Three blasts meant that my dad's crew would work tomorrow.

There was labor unrest during those years, and the president of the labor union was trying to unionize the mines. Mom was very uneasy when Dad left for work carrying a cudgel for "self-defense."

The schoolteacher aunts kept their jobs, but they were paid in "Scrip" or IOUs, and were paid nickels on the dollar when they cashed them. Some of the sons, who had left home for better opportunities in the cities, came back to the farm. Fortunately, most people had a farm connection they could depend upon for food and necessities. What will people do today? Most farms are big commercial operations.

A Confusing Lesson in Money and Banks

Grandfather McKemie gave a silver dollar to each grandchild for birthdays, Christmas, and other times when we had done something to please him. I'd saved most of mine and some of my allowance. We got a nickel each week and I would often end up with six cents. I had learned to charge interest—two cents for every cent whenever friends or my sister needed to borrow money.

I was ten-years-old when I learned that I had lost all of my money when the Bank of Benton was closed by President Roosevelt's declaration of a "Bank Holiday." I kept asking anyone who would listen, "Who got my money? Why don't we get the police to arrest the person who got my money and make them give it back?" But it was all gone.

As the Depression dragged on, the people began to fight back in their own little ways. For example, when the bank officer showed up to auction off a neighbor's property, a conspiracy of sorts was formed. A designated farmer would open the bidding at a very, very low bid, and in spite of the pleas of the frustrated auctioneer, no one else would bid. If a stranger showed up, he soon learned that it would not be healthy to bid. My Dad and others would pool their money to make that first bid. After the auction, the farmer got his plow or tractor back.

And then there was Aunt Effie. She was not a blood relative, but she had lived on an adjoining five acres for eighty-five years. Early in the Depression she borrowed from the bank to fix her leaking roof. She, as did most of us, believed President Hoover when he said, "Prosperity is just around the corner." It wasn't. Her egg and vegetable source of income dried up because people, even in town, raised chickens and plowed up their front yards to grow vegetables. There was no social security program then, and there were no men in her family to work for the CCC or WPA, so she defaulted on her loan from the bank.

Aunt Effie refused to move so the sheriff said he was coming Saturday morning to evict her. Several neighbors and some 7th graders, including me, formed a human chain across her driveway. She stood in front with a big shot gun. When the sheriff saw his "greeting committee" he paused, then retreated.

The papers gleefully said "85-Year Oldster Sends The Posse Packing."

However, they came back unannounced, and took her to the poor house. She died within the month.

In spite of the Depression, my parents gave us a happy and contented childhood. For example, there was a drugstore in town that offered an ice cream cone for five cents with three dips. They had a wide variety of flavors; during the week we would decide on the three flavors only to change our minds the next day for three different flavors.

Our little town also had a movie house, which showed an exciting fantasy characters similar to today's Batman, Green Hornet, and Spider-man every other Saturday. At the end of every serial, they were in dire trouble.

During the next two weeks, we would endlessly try to figure out how they would manage to survive. We waited impatiently for the next Saturday to see whose solution, if any, came closest to the movie version. We also watched the "Lowell Thomas Reports." We were always excited when he showed pictures of the royal Princesses, and for weeks afterward we lived in a fantasy English palace.

On alternate Sundays, we would go to Grandfather and Grandmother Loucks' home. They had five daughters. My mother was the second born. My grandparents lived in a house with a big wrap around porch and a large berry and flower garden taking up half the front yard. Their garden was a child's delight. We could pick raspberries, blueberries, gooseberries, and other kinds of berries to our hearts content.

They had lots of nut trees, such as walnut (the hard kind with the thick green shell that stained your hands). One Sunday when we came up after church, Grandma had been roasting an oven full of peanuts. We ate all of those hot, crunchy peanuts, and most of us had tummy aches that night.

The Loucks were hospitable people. Neighbors would drop in after church just to say hello, but after a few words of encouragement from my grandfather, they would agree to stay for dinner. My cousins and I would begin counting. We knew there were eight seats at the dinner table and the men ate first, then the women, and finally the children. There was always enough food, but often it was quite late before we got to eat. That's when the berries, fruit, and nuts would tide us over until it was our turn.

Young people reading these lines today would probably respond with utter boredom and wonder how we ever got along without televisions, computer games, IPods, organized sports, and parents ferrying us to dance lessons, music lessons, or band practice. Perhaps they are too jaded to enjoy a nickel triple dip ice cream cone.

CHAPTER 3

I'm sitting on the floor in front of a blazing fire surrounded by tapes, articles, pictures, written chapters, and letters written on my Nana's life. One of my biggest problems is in sorting by timeline; some episodes covered a day, while others lasted over a week, or a few months . . . even a decade.

As I looked through the boxes containing tapes, books, and other material that Nana had left in the guest closet of my bedroom, I found a box marked "Teenager." In it were three folders marked "Easter," "Oil Found," and "Illinois Better Speaker's Contest."

Gathering these up, another slipped out: "The Peach Formal."

Each contained a tape of Nana narrating her own story, bringing to light how these experiences further shaped her future.

A Lesson Hard Learned

The Great Depression continued to worsen and cause economic trouble for Everyone, but by 1935, it seemed most people were learning to cope. They were learning to live within their means and to economize in many ways. The massive layoffs, the dislocations, and the lurid news of suicides had been fully exploited. Some newspapers had begun to devote more space to stories about the madman in Germany: Hitler.

The Easter clothes are one example of learning to cope. On the week before Easter, my sister and I got to go shopping to try on and select a complete outfit of "store bought" clothes, right down to our new patent leather shoes and frilly anklets. Then, we would pray that it wouldn't rain on Easter Sunday and ruin our Easter Parade to church. Except for this once a year Easter splurge, my Grandmother Loucks made our clothes. Since I was the oldest girl on both sides, the clothes were made for me, and then handed down.

My grandmother and I had different ideas as to what was "fittin" or stylish. Her idea of a proper hem length was below the knees, and I begged for above the knee. Given her "druthers" my Grandmother would have had my hemline down to my ankles, which was the proper style in her day. For my teaching and speaking career, I wore classic three-piece suits with the skirt length just above the knee. My daughter was able to teach in mini skirts and pant suits and wore a long dress to fancy outings. When I retired, I finally got the courage to "go out" in pant suits. But by that time, my granddaughters were wearing the full and long length skirts again. Thus, the hem length styles had made a full circle in 4 or 5 generations.

I was dark complexioned, but my mother favored the fair "English Rose" complexion. She tried to keep me from becoming "brown as a berry," whatever that means. So, I wore long sleeves, long socks, and a wide-brimmed hat when I went out. Times haven't changed that much, because like many young people today, I tried to create my own style. As soon as I was out of sight, I bunched the dress above my belt to create an above the knee hem; and the long stockings were rolled down to my ankles. I would then bunch the sleeves above my elbows. I must have looked a sight! As I became a teenager, I remember haunting the dry goods store for material and patterns.

Oil Strike

In 1937 the "Great Depression" was over for the McKemie clan. Shell Oil discovered oil in Franklin County! Until then, the majority of the folks were in farming or coal mining. Fortunately, grandfather had great foresight to retain the mineral rights whenever he bought or sold land. This potential windfall caused some anxious searching of county records by farmers and landowners to see if their deeds included these mineral rights. Tempers and resentment ran high for those who discovered they would not be able to share in the oil bounty from their land.

The discovery of oil caused many changes. Soon drilling rigs were all over our county. In our county one-story buildings were the norm, but then tall, lighted rigs began dotting the landscape, changing our entire view of the land. Then the population doubled and new housing sprang up for the first time in a decade. Empty, abandoned homes were opened and occupied by "oil people."

The sudden, almost double number of students in our school necessitated the hiring of new teachers by a school district that couldn't pay regular teacher's salaries. My "school teacher aunts" had been getting Scrip IOU's. The "oil students" had traveled and lived all over the country, when most of us hadn't been out of Franklin County. They were both awe-inspiring and frightening. Turf battles erupted between the local boys and the "oil boys," escalating their differences. The oil kids had a lot more money than we did, but gradually they left town as oil the wells started rhythmic pumping, and didn't need so many handlers. Those who were left assimilated into our town, and they surely did help our football team.

As the oil wells started to produce, we began to receive royalty checks regularly. Being Scottish by nature, and not quite sure this new-found prosperity would last, we began to slowly buy things that we had missed during the recession. Then we began to take the money out of the mattress and deposit it back in the bank. Shell Oil paid heavy taxes, which helped the school district's funding. Even the people who didn't receive oil royalties prospered, because they were employed to help service the new oil industry.

A related story by way of our new prosperity: One Christmas, we all received furs. Mine was made of five mink pelts, artistically joined together to make a stole. I still have it! Mom received a warm coat, her first in eighteen years. It had a fur collar and cuffs. I still wear mine occasionally to remind me of the great oil discovery in Franklin County.

Illinois Best Speaker

Off that track I remember another story. One of the highlights of my high school years was something I refer to as "The Illinois Better Speaker's Contest." From an early age, I was speaking in public at various community events. I don't remember how I got started except my grandfather played a key role. One of my earliest memories was being lifted onto grandfather's shoulders to give a Mother's Day recitation. On alternate Sundays, we would visit the Loucks' home. Grandfather was a deacon in a small community church. He was always scheduling me to recite a piece for Sunday services.

He would tell all his neighbors to come to church and hear his granddaughter.

I would have to memorize a new piece each time I went.

Also, every Saturday for about two years, I would recite a tear-jerker for the WCTU, (Women's Christian Temperance Union) on their radio program. This group was partially responsible for, and the passage of, the Prohibition Laws (no liquor sold in public).

These experiences gave me poise and confidence. So I entered the Illinois Better Speaker's contest in my junior year of high school. I had to write a twenty minute speech on patriotism. This was a national contest, sponsored by the American Legion. Each state was to send their best speaker to the finals. My parents and Grandfather Loucks followed me to each level: local, county, district, and finally the state contest. Those were nail biting and anxious times for all of us. When I won the State, they were proud as peacocks. However, I lost the national contest. A boy from New York won. Grandfather Loucks proudly said, "I should have been with you."

Peach Formal

During my senior year of high school, I faced an important crossroads and a wake-up call in the form of The Peach Formal. All through school, especially high school, the town's judge's son, Bob, and I competed for grades. Grades were very important to me because the top student received a 4-year scholarship and that meant that I could go to college if I won. The teachers and many of our schoolmates were aware of this informal competition. As was traditional, on the last day of our senior year an assembly was held to recognize the academic records of the soon-to-be graduates. On this day, tensions were high. The principal began by calling students to the stage, starting with 10th place. Then he called 9th, 8th, and so on until he got to 2nd place. The assembly grew very quiet; neither Bob nor I had been called up. Then second place was called: "Bob Hart." Cheering broke out; the Judge's son had been outranked by the farmer's daughter! As quiet was restored, I walked up on shaking legs to accept the title of Valedictorian and the college scholarship. You would think this would be the happiest day of my life, but as it turned out it was to be the saddest day; up to that point anyway.

Bob had previously invited me to the Senior Prom. After the assembly, I rushed home to prepare for the big night. The beautiful Peach Formal dress with matching shoes hung in my closet. The hairdresser and make-up artist were arranged. The aunts had excitedly chosen all the proper accessories . . . then the phone rang. At about 5 p.m. Bob's mother called and said he was "sick" and could not go to the prom.

My family was outraged by this slight and I was crushed. My uncle, nearest to me in age, offered to take me. Even my dear Father offered to get a tux and escort me. My cousin, Leroy, called to say his date had reluctantly agreed that I could join them in an awkward threesome. I refused all offers and stayed home on this important occasion.. "My Senior Prom."

I vowed that I would never, ever again, let a boy know I was smart. Dramatic, maybe, but for a young lady of my tender age, appropriate. Twenty-five years later I saw the beautiful Peach Formal in its protective covering hanging in my parent's closet. I don't know what ever happened to it. That was a lesson hard learned.

CHAPTER 4

It's raining again. We had three days respite. I used those rainless days to work out the pent up energy from over a week of heavy downpour. We planted two more trees, a dwarf apple and another fast growing pine. Ironically, when we bought the lot it was heavily treed, but almost all the trees had to be cut down to make way for the roads and foundations of the house. Luckily, we sold much of the lumber and created a tree replacement fund. But now that inclement weather has confined me to the house, I'll begin to write and transcribe again. This tape talks about people I know or heard Nana talk about. I also learned something about her and the handsome young navy cadet who became my beloved Grandfather.

The acerbic remarks of the history professor changed her career and thus her life. But I'll let her tell you about these life changing events.

The Cadet & the History Professor

With my scholarship in hand, I enrolled at Illinois State University in Carbondale, Illinois, about fifty miles away. I wasn't quite brave enough to stray too far. At the university there was a feeling of rushing to get things done before the United States joined the war in December, 1941. The young men especially were debating whether they should volunteer to get the billet of their choice, or to get as many credits as they could before they were drafted.

The campus became a training ground for the armed services and soon many men in uniform could be seen in classes. We knew they were there for a very short time, so we girls were cautioned not to try to make lasting relationships. We were mobilizing to arm the Allies and employment picked up as factories and ship building yards re-opened to supply the Allies. That war ended the Depression. Our armed forces were growing and many college men were joining up. Our university followed the University of Chicago's accredited program, which stated that a student could get credit for classes *if they* could pass the final exam. I "examed" out of all my freshman classes and began my sophomore year. The campus was so big and the large student body awed me. I wondered how I was even going to get known or noticed.

Soon after, there was an announcement for a talent show for new students with a "mixer" afterwards. I couldn't dance or sing; my only talent was public speaking and that didn't seem very exciting. So I went to the Dramatics Department and they decided to help me. They fitted me out in a long, slinky red dress a long black wig, and more make-up than I had ever worn before. They taught me how to sing the words to "Ahapala" and rehearsed the sexy movements to the song over and over with me, and how to use a long stem red rose effectively. The night of the talent show, they supervised the recording so that it came off without a hitch. When the song ended, I threw the red rose into the audience. It worked! The drama department and I shared the applause. When I came out the door, several stage-door-Johnnies were waiting and I had a wonderful time at the mixer.

As one of many students from a small town protective environment, I did not use my best judgment during my first year, and soon got into trouble. I was staying out late, getting on "report," and ignoring my studies. The stagedoor-Johnnies were keeping me busy and I was lapping it up.

Then disaster struck.

A call into the Dean's office, a threat to cancel my scholarship and send me home in disgrace, woke me up. I buckled down and worked very hard to get off probation.

My New Man

During the fall of 1942, my parents started driving down on alternate Sundays and brought me food. Mom was a fabulous cook and the farm provided all the fruits and vegetables I needed. Students in the other houses on campus realized that if they came by the girl's dorm around 2 p.m. they might get a treat.

One particular Sunday, my folks had brought bushels of red apples. As several of us stood around eating them, the most handsome man I had ever seen strolled by in his Cadet's uniform. On an impulse, I threw him an apple.

He caught it and walked on. We girls "oohd and aahhd." And the men said, "It's just the uniform." He came back the next day and asked for the girl who threw the apple.

While he waited at the dorm, my roommate and others helped me to quick change my clothes, put on make-up, fix my hair, then sent me down to meet the handsome officer.

Our dorm had a wide veranda with swings, chairs, etc. We sat on a swing for two. He thanked me for the apple and we talked for a while. James Radford Belt was from the tiny town of Shawneetown, Illinois. James told me that two years previously when he got his high school degree, his folks couldn't afford to send him to college. However, because he was 6' 5," he got a basketball scholarship. Then, he worked in a restaurant for food and stayed in a cold room over a garage for shelter. As we chatted, he told me he was in training to be an aircraft pilot and had been assigned to our university to study psychology. To explain his major he said, "Because most young men were being drafted, I joined the Navy and was assigned as a pilot on the 'flat tops.' Being a teacher in civilian life, they sent me from college to college to learn all I needed to know to help the other young pilots in training. That's how I ended up here to learn psychological theory to help stressed flyers." He would stay at the university until the end of 1943. He also mentioned Einstein's theory of Relativity. The next day I went to the library to read everything I could about Einstein so I would not be so dumb if he ever came again. James Radford Belt started dropping by after classes frequently. As the months flew by, I was completely smitten and head over heels in love. By the end of the first semester, we had become an 'item' and frequently discussed plans for the future. On Christmas, Jim came to my home and he and my father took a long walk; evidently they came to an understanding. On a beautiful spring day in March of 1943, we decided to bike somewhere with no particular place in mind. After about two hours we saw this little country church, and decided to have our picnic on the church grounds. After we had finished eating and Jim was repacking our picnic basket, he said he found something he had forgotten, he pulled out a ringbox and offered it to me. He simply said "Will you?" After a moment's hesitation I nodded. Then, as if by one accord, we stood and walked through the open doors of the church. All those many years ago, seventy years to be exact, most churches left the doors open to offer a place of hope and comfort to families devastated by the war. We walked into the cool, sacred interior of the church, knelt at the altar and sealed our future.

As we began the second semester I started a much accelerated program. Our university allowed "unlimited cuts" to those on the Dean's List.

I signed up for two classes every hour, attended intermittently, and took the exams, thus I finished my sophomore and junior year in one year.

Jim and I set the date for our marriage on June 6, 1943, my 20th birthday. The reactions to our wedding plans were far from encouraging. "You are too young; you haven't finished school yet; you're ruining your life; he's too old; he's in the Navy in a dangerous job; he's too poor."

Even the psychology professor got into the act. He called me up after class. "Don't marry that man, Virginia Lee." He predicted that the marriage wouldn't last one day over six months. Jim and I used to say we wished he were alive when we celebrated our 53rd anniversary. Also, my favorite uncle called from Africa where he was stationed as a doctor and said, "If you won't get married and have "forty-eleven kids," I'll take you to Europe when I get back home." But when we convinced everybody that we were going to get married, they reluctantly began to plan the wedding.

My Aunt Susie spearheaded the plans. She selected pale lavender and pale yellow as the colors for a June wedding. All the flowers, bridesmaids dresses, ribbons, invitations were in those colors. My Baptist church was building a new sanctuary and the minister was pressuring the contractors to finish before my wedding date.

Then the Navy ordered Jim to report to Northwestern University on May 25th. We insisted on being married on Sunday, May 23rd. I now realize how we inconvenienced so many people. Relatives who had arranged to travel, which was very difficult during gas rationing and restricted war time travel, couldn't change their plans. Contractors complained they had to finish the main chapel out of order. The women's missionary society decorated the church, the florist had to rush order the flowers, and the right bra couldn't be found, so my roommate had to manufacture one on Sunday morning from the ribbon on the wedding gifts!

Finally the church was ready, the attendants were in town, and Aunt Susie breathed a sigh of relief. The church was really beautiful with lavender and yellow decorations everywhere. Then Jim inadvertently blew it all.

The florist was cued to show Jim a lovely bridal bouquet of one lavender orchid and two smaller yellow orchids with lots of ribbons. However, when the apologetic florist delivered the bridal bouquet that Jim had selected, it was a huge gaudy mass of red carnations. Aunt Susie went ballistic! Almost everyone felt that it would ruin the whole decor. I sighed and agreed, but said that I had to carry it because Jim had selected it. Aunt Susie never did forgive him. Years later when I asked him about it, he said that the florist had shown him one bouquet with two or three puny flowers, but he wanted to get the most flowers he could with the money he had. Hence, the red carnations.

We spent our wedding night at my grandparents and believe it or not, they put us in separate rooms! I spent the night in nervous anticipation and dread. It felt like l had waited for hours. Much later I found out that Grandpa had taken him to the woodshed and given him a verbal licking about NOT going into my room. I finally fell asleep waiting for the door to open. Grandpa was worried that I might get pregnant and gave a ton of reasons why that was about the worst thing that might happen to me. Jim left the next day for Northwestern University near Chicago. I stayed on at CSU to finish my senior year.

Since I had unlimited cuts, I signed up for several classes during the same hours, creating a full day and evening of classes. History was my major, so I presented my history advisor with a schedule of twenty-four semester hours in a three-month summer session. He refused to sign, saying, "I will not sign anyone's death certificate." So I took it to another professor during the harried registration period and he signed it without taking a look.

To fill my schedule, I signed up for a class in Money and Banking. I was hooked!

It was the most interesting class I had ever taken. Realizing that I was going to need references when I started job hunting, I went to a history advisor. He said, "I had to give you an A because you earned it, but I do not have to give you a reference. You seldom came to class and when you were there, you paid scant attention. Besides you wouldn't make a good historian. You are in too much of a hurry and you look to the future instead of the past. I can't imagine you sitting in some musty basement patiently looking for the middle name of a man long dead and long forgotten." I was deeply hurt and I rushed across campus and signed up for a business major. Although history was my first choice, I realized the department was not sympathetic to my fast-track schedule. So I switched my major to business. That meant taking more classes than I had planned on. Even though I resented the history professor and the department, I bless him now. I wonder what my life would have been had I remained a history major. By the end of the fall semester, January 1944, I lacked only six credits to get my degree. With the cooperation of my business professors, I arranged to take these courses by correspondence.

It was with mixed emotions of fear and anticipation that I boarded the train for the 300-mile journey to Chicago, the Windy City. I knew no one there and Jim was twenty-five miles away at Northwestern. He had hoped to meet me but the train schedule did not mesh with his. I had the address of a "sitting room" unit he had rented for me. It was about one block off Michigan Avenue near the Chicago Water Tower. He saw me every other weekend from Saturday afternoon to Sunday afternoon. Not much of a honeymoon or way to start a marriage, but we enjoyed our time together.

As the train traveled further and further away from home toward the unknown, I became more and more agitated. The train was loaded with young servicemen; they were loud, boisterous, laughing perhaps to cover their nervousness. Perhaps they, like me, were uncertain about their future.

As luck would have it, I was sitting next to an older man who was calmly reading. I tried to read, but couldn't concentrate. Perhaps he sensed my fear, and so introduced himself. "I'm Silas, a diamond merchant. I've lived in Chicago for most of my life."

As we chatted, I asked all types of questions about Chicago. Perhaps I should say I talked during the last hour of our journey. Maybe I talked too much, revealed too much to a perfect stranger. At any rate, he knew about Jim.

He knew I wanted to go to a main library where I would most likely find the textbooks I needed to finish my degree.

"I have a job interview at the Continental Bank at 3:30 this afternoon," I said. When we exited the train, out of kindness (or for some other reason?) he grabbed a taxi and took me to the library. Since I didn't have a library card, he checked them out in his name. Then because time was running short, we grabbed another taxi to the Continental Bank.

The Navy had commandeered the top floors of the building and I was to report to the 5th floor where the personnel department was located. He escorted me there and as I was being whisked off for the job interview, he tipped his hat and said, "see you." I was concentrating so much on what I would say at the interview that I couldn't even remember if I had thanked him.

Once in the personnel department, I filled out reams of papers, answered many questions, and went to several floors for different tests. An hour or so later, I got the job and was directed to return the next day.

I planned to take the elevator down to the reception room where I had left my suitcase behind the receptionist desk. When the elevator doors opened, I was startled to see Silas still waiting there. Alarm bells started going off in my head, so I made a snap decision and rode the elevator down to the street level.

The bank occupied the entire block, so when I came out I was completely disoriented. And was it cold, a bone chilling cold that is common in Chicago in January. After many requests for directions to anyone who would stop long enough to listen, I found the correct bus stop on Michigan Avenue.

The howling, blowing wind whistling down that broad avenue gave meaning to the term Windy City. Thank goodness I had taken my coat and purse with me during the interviews.

Finally, I caught the right bus and the driver told me the correct stop. It was dark and I was scared when I found the rather ominous looking brownstone where Jim had rented a room for me. As I walked up those steps to a dimly lit entry, I prayed that someone would open the door for me.

Fortunately, the building manager met me, and escorted me to my room.

"Thank you for your kindness," I said to her. Then I sighed. "I've forgotten my luggage at the bank where I'll start working tomorrow." She smiled and left my room. A few minutes later she returned with a nightie for me to wear that night.

As I lay on my lumpy bed, still cold and very hungry, I was thankful that I had successfully navigated my first day in Chicago. I was thankful that I had a new job and, yes, I was thankful for Silas. He was a godsend. I wouldn't have managed without him. Had I been unfair to him? How long did he wait?

What did he think had happened to me? Or was he one of those people I needed to avoid? Had my guardian angel at the last minute kept me from a bad experience that I was too young and too naive to handle? I never found the answers.

CHAPTER 5

This fifth chapter confuses me. She titles it the pool and the brown dress which makes me wonder what relationship there can be between a pool and a dress. I thought you used swimsuits in pools, not dresses. But let's read this chapter and find out what she meant.

The Pool & the Brown Dress

When I arrived at the bank the next morning, I reported to the pool.

Almost all new hires started in the pool. From there, poolies were assigned by the Officer of the Pay to departments in need of typists, filers, and gofers in general. The Navy had appropriated the top fifteen (or was it twenty-five?) floors of the Illinois Continental Bank. Thus a poolie, as we were called, never knew where or for whom they would be working. Everyone seemed hurried, impatient, and not always kind to us who were at the bottom of the scale.

After two weeks, I was determined to get out of the pool. Twice I had been assigned to the testing department. There they administered tests to all navy personnel, and based upon test scores they filled the request of field commanders for mechanics, radiomen, gunners, spotters, and all types of specialists, including unassigned personnel or "cannon fodder" they were called. The work challenged me, and I hoped to be assigned permanently to that department. I asked (begged) the officer of the day to send me to that department every time she could. She was surprised and said that Commander Rothman was considered a hard task master.

Soon, I was reporting to that department almost daily. I always tried to do more and better than was required. Eventually, I attracted the attention of Commander Rothman, and when he needed help he asked for me. Soon after, he requested that I be assigned to his department. Wow, I was out of the pool!

One of his requirements for all new employees was for them to take tests like the GED. These were given to all Navy men who came through our department. Later, he called me into his office and told me I had achieved the 2nd highest score on the GED out of all the Navy men in the 5th District. From then on, I was rapidly promoted to more responsible positions. Part of my job was to collate the test scores and to assign the sailors to the position their scores showed they would be best suited and happiest.

Camaraderie sprang up among those of us in the department and I gradually made friends. One girl, Mary Carmackce, from a large Italian family, often invited me to her home. On my birthday, June 6, 1944, the department threw a party for me complete with cake. Of course, the highlight of my life was the alternate weekends when my new husband could visit me.

Jim was on a very intensive schedule at Northwestern University. I remember that he was required to pass an aerodynamics class after three months of studying that usually took one year. Our time together was so short. We would spend Saturday noon to Sunday noon every two weeks going out to eat or enjoying the spring and early balmy Chicago weather in the small patch of garden behind my brownstone building.

At work, I was progressing rapidly and was very content for the most part.

Among my duties was administering the GED test. Recruits who had just spent three months in boot camp were bused in to take the test. Usually there were about a hundred at a time filing into a large auditorium set up with desk chairs. Monitors and sailors assigned to our department distributed the tests and pencils. These monitors were to prevent cheating, keep order, and to run a tight ship according to the Commander's orders. After everyone was ready, I would walk out on an elevated stage and give instructions and start the testing.

Among my scant supply of clothes that I had been able to bring with me was a brown A-line dress with brass buttons designed to enhance my breasts and slim my waist. I had matching brown shoes and the Commander had been able to procure nylons. About every third or fourth day I'd get a call or a note telling me that a test was scheduled and he would always add "and wear the brown dress." I grew to hate those words because I knew what was going to happen.

Imagine a room full of young boys just out of boot camp, who hadn't seen a woman in months. There I was walking out on the stage in my short, form-fitting brown dress. The monitors immediately pounced on any recruit who whistled or did anything disrespectful. They were put on report and their test marked with an F. Then they would be assigned to the lowest, most menial rank in the Navy. This happened week after week. I finally told Jim what was happening. He was incensed and threatened to do something about it. But before he could get himself and me into trouble, he was transferred to Great Lakes Naval Base in northern Illinois. I resigned and followed him.

As I left Chicago, I put the brown dress in a Salvation Army bin.

CHAPTER 6

I had never heard Nana talk about how she and Papa felt about the birth of my mother, or what their economic situation was like on August 6, 1945. So let's enjoy Nana's story together.

First Lady, First Baby

Great Lakes Naval Station, the nation's largest naval base, was located in NE Illinois with Wisconsin as its northern boundary and Lake Michigan on the East. My memory of Great Lakes is of the endless cold, even during the summer.

The Navy had transferred a branch of Naval Air Force to Great Lakes and Jim's job involved the indoctrination and placement of airmen, sort of a way station on their way to the Pacific arena. Since he would be living on base, we had to find a place for me. It turned out to be a third floor walk-up in a large house belonging to the banker's mother in Waukegan, the largest town near the base.

Ms Etherton was a kind and generous person, a grandmotherly type. When I would come in from work, she would say, "I made too much soup," or stew, or a casserole, and add, "Would you please share it with me? I hate waste." Thus, she made me feel that I was doing her a favor instead of sponging off her. She had very definite opinions about most things, including sex. One day she asked me if my husband and I wanted children now. I explained that we wanted to wait until we and the world were more settled before we started our family. Then she said,

"Sex should only happen when you want children. Any other time is a sin." After that, there was many a Saturday afternoon Jim and I turned up the volume on the Chicago Symphony Orchestra in my little walk-up rooms.

A New Direction

I needed to find a job, both to give me something to do and because we could use the money. So I applied for and was hired by the Waukegan school district to teach Art. I smiled, recalling Grandfather hiring an art teacher and a music teacher to improve my chances for a straight "A" in junior high. Now the art lessons could be put to use.

I have always enjoyed teaching, and I believe it was because my first experience was so satisfying. I traveled from school to school for two lessons per week. My classes were welcomed by the students as a break from regular classes. And what young person doesn't like using pencil and paint to express their inner emotions? I taught only color, shape, and how to get perceptions, then left the subject up to their imagination.

Jim and I began looking for a home nearer my work and the Base. We found a quaint, one bedroom mobile home that we could afford. Our first home! We papered and painted and used bright colors throughout. I was trying to learn to cook and keep house. During my years at home, my mother taught my sister and she became a fabulous cook. I, on the other hand, kept all the "books" and was more guided by my father who treated me as the son he wished he had.

I remember Thanksgiving, 1944. We wanted a traditional turkey dinner, so Jim bought a turkey at the commissary, and I began reading about turkey preparation. Alas, we discovered that his turkey was too big for our little oven in our home. What to do? Jim solved it by taking the turkey over to a navy cook in our park and persuaded him to roast our turkey along with the hundreds he was roasting for the men on the Base. We had a perfectly browned turkey for our first Thanksgiving in our first home.

A New Life

Soon after, a life-changing event occurred. I became pregnant. How did it happen? We had been so careful and had practiced abstinence for the most part. Finally, at the doctor's insistence that we fix a date, we remembered the football game in December between the University of Illinois and the Navy teams. It was bitterly cold and snowing. Although we left early, we were chilled through and through. Our little home, we learned, was not as weather proofed as it should have been, so we went to bed to huddle and cuddle as we warned up. That must have been the time.

I was in denial for the first months, but finally accepted the truth and began to plan for the arrival of a third person in our lives. I continued to work as an art teacher, and I was able to wear my artist's smock so that neither the students nor school administrators knew I was pregnant. Fortunately, I was seldom sick and I watched my diet carefully so that I gained less than ten pounds. After school was out in June, the waiting game began.

I realized early on that if I wanted a career in the field of business, I had to learn a lot about accounting and taxes. During my previous school training, I had not taken those classes. So with time on my hands I enrolled in a correspondence school. It became a matter of pride to see how rapidly I could study and return my answers to the instructors for correction. Finally, on August 6, 1945 our daughter, Patricia Leah Belt, was born in the naval hospital in Waukegan, Illinois. The doctors and nurses must have thought we were strange parents. Jim's first comment to the doctor was, "Will she get her shape back?" and about four hours after Pat's birth, I was sitting up and studying my tax texts.

August 6, 1945 was also the day the atomic bomb destroyed Hiroshima, Japan. Jim said there was a lot of rejoicing in the streets that night, because it appeared that the war was almost over. Hitler had committed suicide in April and German generals had sued for peace. Surely Japan would now follow. About a week later, and after another devastating bomb had destroyed Nagasaki, Japan sued for peace.

Jim and I took our first baby to our little home, and frankly, I was scared during the day. I had read a lot of books on caring for a baby, but it was so different in reality. Pat was such a tiny little girl (4 lbs 6oz) and I was terrified I would do something wrong. Fortunately, she was a good baby and except for a bout with impetigo, which she caught in the hospital, she was seldom ill. We gradually began to know each other and to fall in love.

The war was over, but the base personnel department was as busy, if not more so, than ever. The thousands of men and women who had been drafted over the four year time period of the war now wanted out as quickly as possible.

We got a scare in December of 1945; the Navy had a policy of transferring personnel every six months. Jim had to report to O.G.U. (Outgoing Unit). For two weeks, he was restricted to Base, ready to ship out to some unknown destination. I was alone with a four-month-old baby, not knowing what was going to happen. Fortunately, he was reassigned to Great Lakes! His job was very stressful and harried as he tried to cope with bus load after bus load arriving each day filled with troops eager and impatient to be discharged. Because of Jim's involvement in the discharge process for others, we realized that his own discharge was somewhere in the distant future.

With $2,000 borrowed from my parents, we bought a bigger and better mobile home from a discharged officer. I continued to care for our daughter and took correspondence classes that I thought would be needed for my future.

Finally, in August of 1946, Jim was discharged.

California, here we come!

CHAPTER 7

As I rummaged through the next box, I pondered about the meaning of Nana's notes that were subtitled, "The Lost Year," "The GI Bill," "The Cracker Box," "Mathematics," and "Two Degrees and a Half." What did all of these have in common? Did they help or hinder her toward becoming a pioneer woman in a man's world of finance? Well, there's only one way to find out. Transcribe the tapes and put them in book form, and fulfill the oft repeated, "You ought to write a book."

California Delays

From 1946 to 1948, there was a large migration of ex-servicemen to California, the land of milk, honey, and opportunity. We wanted to join that migration. After several months setting up our affairs, selling our home, and paying off our debt to my parents, we headed to Southern Illinois to reacquaint ourselves with our families. After about a month, during which time we took a trip with college friends to Mexico, we finally headed for California.

However, we only got as far as St. Louis, Missouri, when we realized we had to stop and get a job; we simply did not have the necessary funds. Our savings for the California trip were dwindling faster than a snowball in a hothouse. We missed the fifteen-cent-a-gallon gas, the low priced food on the Base, the entertainment and all the freebees we received from the Navy. Now the real world of economics caught up with us. Jim found a job teaching, and I continued to care for our daughter and take correspondence courses. We considered it a 'lost year.' Jim and I took time to project realistic budget projections. With a sigh of resignation after he completed his contract, we decided to return to Illinois where we had some roots. After settling down in another mobile home, we both enrolled at the University of Illinois. Jim had the GI Bill, which paid for his tuition and some toward our cost of living. He majored in educational administration.

After several weeks, I found a job teaching high school algebra for the Urbana School District. Wow! That was going to be challenging as math was *not* my forte. Eventually things settled down. Jim was studying for his Masters in Education, our daughter was enrolled in the university play school, and I had started taking courses to get my Master's degree.

We moved into University housing that had been constructed for the large number of married couples studying under the GI bill. We tried to maintain a normal kind of family life, but that wasn't always possible. For example: Jim and I had always gone to bed together. Yet at this time, I would wait until he was asleep and then slip out of bed and study the next day's Algebra lesson. I had never concentrated beyond the bare minimum so now I had to study each day's lesson to keep ahead of my students.

Among the many letters, articles, and appointments I have received during my teaching career, the one that I value the most is a note from the mother of one of my Algebra students. It appeared to be torn from a page of a student's workbook and said, "I thought that I had heard everything a student could say about a teacher, but our middle son surprised us last night and said, 'I bet we've got the best Algebra teacher in the country – no, she's the best teacher in the whole world!' I thought you'd like to know."

I must have done OK though because I received a "superior" rating in my year-end evaluation and was rehired for the 2nd year.

That summer, I enrolled at the university in business and economics.

As I noted before, the university had constructed several temporary houses on campus to accommodate the large number of GI bill students and their families. These houses, which were called cracker boxes by those of us who lived in them, were hastily and badly constructed. Splinters were a common malady.

Another cracker box family had a daughter the same age as Patty.

Since she was a stay-at-home mom, we hired her to care for Patty. She was a good seamstress, and she dressed the girls alike so they looked like a couple of dolls. I learned to knit and made them matching clothes as well. We also enrolled Patty in the university "training school," where teacher education majors got hands-on experience.

It was during this time that I learned to get by on four hours (or less) sleep per night. I was teaching algebra full-time, five days a week, took college courses nights, weekends, and summers. I tried to spend time at night as a companion to my husband and mother to my daughter. Then after they went to bed, I studied for my math classes the next day and for my college classes the next night. That habit carried over even until today. It's 3:45 a.m., Saturday night as I write this, and I'll probably be up at 8 a.m. for church tomorrow, even though I'm eighty-eight-years-old. Wow!

After two years, Jim and I had each acquired enough credits to earn our Master's Degrees. A reporter, prowling campus and gathering material for a book on "Education: Family Style," featured our story and took a picture of Jim and I in our master's hat and gown, and Patty in her long white graduation dress from nursery school. He titled it "Two Degrees and a Half." That picture appeared in several newspapers.

Now, California here we come—with advanced degrees in our hands.

CHAPTER 8

It's raining again . . . Not the hard driving rain of winter, but a gentle rain, like a spring mist. But, it is enough to drive me in and give me the incentive to continue on with Nana's life story. This next chapter she wrote seems intriguing according to the title. Let's read it together.

A Big Fish & 24 Chickens

"The best laid plans of mice and men going all astray."

—Robbie Burns, Irish Poet

With two Master's Degrees in our hands, Jim and I planned to leave for California. For weeks, we'd studied maps and planned a route that would allow us to see the must-see sights between Illinois and California. We decided that we had a month before we would reach Orange County, where we had been promised jobs.

Then, opportunity struck! It was too good to pass up.

In Shawneetown, Illinois, the principal of the high school and County Superintendent of Schools (he held two positions), was leaving for two years on a mission for his church. Jim's father, who lived on a farm outside Shawneetown, urged him to apply.

With our car and a small U-Haul already loaded with our worldly possessions, mostly books, we headed south instead of west.

We had a successful meeting with the Board and Principal Mead. We even rented the Mead's home for two years. We were on our way!

Shawneetown is one of the oldest towns in Illinois. Seated on the Ohio River, it was an early port and was harassed by river pirates. It had the distinction of refusing a loan to Chicago that small settlement on Lake Michigan which it thought would never survive. Shawneetown hasn't grown much in the last hundred years, unlike Chicago. It is a small farming and fishing community. A large state park located up and down the Ohio attracted visitors for the catfish and restored paddle boats that offer dinner, fiddlers and mind challenging riddles. I remember several family outings there. My Grandmother Loucks would deep fry cornbread-basted catfish, which I remember with longing, even to this day. For my husband, this experience would be worth gold to his resume. A high school principal and County Superintendent of Schools—wow! The high school had an enrollment that averaged 900 to 950 students, depending upon planting and harvest time.

There were also four grade schools in the county.

Big Fish

Principal J. R. Belt hired me to teach history and civics. Finally, all of those years of history reading and study could be put to use. During the second semester, I introduced a class in Economics 101. It had to be adjusted for a farm economy. For example, the town had a small, once-a-week newspaper. I asked the editor if it carried market quotations, meaning quotes such as IBM and General Motors. He replied, "Of course, see page 6." Yes, there were quotes—prices for hogs, cows, wheat, corn, and others. I just smiled and shook my head. The drugstore carried the Sunday Chicago Tribune, which I depended on to monitor the small portfolio I had started with the class. I tried to order the Wall Street Journal, but they didn't deliver to our small town.

We soon discovered that we were very big fish, in a very small pond.

We were known by everybody in the county, and we had to always appear dressed-to-the-nines as befitted the principal and his wife. Even at home,

I could expect guests at any time, especially on Saturday when farmers came to town to shop and sell their crops at the Farmer's Market. They would bring choice tomatoes, peaches, and more. I felt that I always needed to have a crock of ice tea made in the summertime and a pot of apple cider ready in the winter.

We were expected to join the church and attend all county meetings.

Jim was asked to be a judge at 4-H Fairs and I was asked to vote for the best quilts, pies, and pickles at the County Fair. That was rather ironic for I had never baked a pie, canned anything, or quilted.

If you have never attended a county fair, you should. They are a piece of Americana that can be traced to our European ancestry. The competition is fierce for the best rose, pig, rabbit, pie, or cake. You'll also see a hundred more things that men, women, and especially children could wear, grow, or make to show off their skill. More importantly, though, it was a joyful joining of the community.

Jim soon joined the Masonic Order; his father was a 32nd degree Mason. This triggered a memory, causing me to contemplate my wedding rings. After we were engaged, we went to visit his folks, and I was wearing my engagement ring. I didn't know much about diamonds and was happy with it; however, Jim's father had his own opinion. Mr. Belt told his son, "She is too fine a lady for you to give her such a cheap diamond." He then took from his Masonic ring, a flawless blue/white diamond, and gave it to Jim—for me! It became a part of my engagement/wedding ring ensemble and still I am wearing it sixty-five years later.

I joined the local "sewing bee" and learned to knit and crochet. I made several outfits for Patty and remember one in particular. It was a white crocheted skirt and a blouse made from a beautiful blue parachute silk that Jim had somehow brought back from his days as a Naval Air Force officer. I still have a picture of my beautiful daughter, four at the time, wearing it.

Another advantage to living in Shawneetown was living within easy driving distance from both sets of relatives. For the first time, Patty got to know her grandparents, aunts, uncles, and cousins, especially her cousin Donetta, my sister's daughter who was very dear to me.

Our house had a huge freezer in the basement for good reason. When either set of the families had a baked ham, fresh steaks or hamburger, or slaughtered a whole pig, they would bring some from their freezer to ours.

Back then, it was just something families did so everyone had enough. Wow, we did live high-off-the-hog, so to speak. Jim's folks kept us supplied with vegetables and eggs, and after church we would find a Sunday chicken, delivered pan ready when we got home.

Oh! Speaking of chickens, I'm reminded of an episode that I laugh about to this day, but cried about at the time. The very hectic twelve-hour experience began on a day at the beginning of our second year. We picked up our daughter from Jones' Play School. Jo Jones, a nice grandmotherly type, cared for our daughter and the daughter of the music teacher while we were at work. But a startling sight greeted us when we got home. There were several coops of squawking chickens on our front porch. They were hot, crowded, and had been doing what chickens do best for no telling how long. Whew, what a mess! What a stench!

While I got a bite to eat and got Pat ready for bed, Jim explained what he thought had happened. That weekend, he had talked to one of our local farmers. He casually mentioned that he probably needed to get some chicken for the freezer. The chicken farmer asked, "How many?"

Jim replied, "Oh a dozen or so." And there they were twenty-four unhappy chickens and two equally unhappy recipients. Jim had never killed a chicken and I had never dressed one. He didn't remember which farmer he had talked to and we couldn't return them, so let the assembly line begin. First, Jim tried several ways to behead the chickens, none to successfully. I cut off legs and wings and then didn't know where to go from there. It was gruesome, certainly not the world of academia we were used to!

About midnight, one got loose and Jim was chasing a badly maimed chicken all over the backyard. Understandably, it was protesting loudly. A neighbor, disturbed by the ruckus, came to see what was wrong. He looked with dismay at the pandemonium, went home to dress and returned with the proper tools. He quietly and expeditiously finished the beheading.

Those chickens were piling up faster than I could process them. We didn't have enough big pots to heat the water to make the feathers come out easily. About 5 am, in desperation, I used the neighbor's cleaver to quarter them, and put them in freezer bags—feathers and all! I reasoned that later when thawed, I could deal with the damage one at a time.

The next morning, Jim put on his Superintendent of Schools hat, having decided to visit one of the grade schools in the Hinterland. On the way out, he stopped by the house and gathered up heads, legs and feathers, and I never did know what he did with them. Thus ended the saga of the twenty-four chickens . . . almost. Months later, we were still finding stray feathers to remind us of that folly.

Moving On

The rest of the year passed quickly and uneventfully. We never again worked where we felt more liked and appreciated by the students and the community. Jim added basketball coaching to his other duties. The math teacher, who had been the coach, left for greener pastures. The little lady who replaced him hardly qualified. At 6 feet 5 inches, Jim had played in high school on a basketball scholarship. The basketball team did so-so, which was OK, considering that the best (tallest) players often missed school to work at home on the family farm. They also couldn't practice after school because they had to catch the bus.

I helped organize the club Shawnee Maidens. We met for a monthly pow wow and sponsored dances and other entertainments. Even with all of our duties, Jim and I were constantly aware that our tenure was ending soon.

Principal Mead was coming back to his job and his home. Where would we go? California?

At a meeting of school administrators, Jim learned that the Davenport, Iowa district had an opening. So he applied and got the job. I didn't know what I would do, but his salary was so good that we didn't have to worry. At the end of the school year, we said a sad farewell to all our friends and family in Southern Illinois, and heading north instead of west, continued our adventure.

One last note on those chickens. We cleaned and aired out the freezer and put anything we had left in my parent's freezer. I often wonder how my mother reacted when she opened a package of quartered, partially-feathered chickens.

CHAPTER 9

I have just finished transcribing the tape for this chapter. If I was in awe of Nana's accomplishments before, now I am almost speechless in admiration for her ingenuity, innovation, and imagination that enabled her to turn an ordinary, ho-hum event into an extraordinary success, bringing honor to her employer and reward to herself.

Perhaps you have noticed, as I have, how Nana was able to take some experience from her earlier life and use that to achieve greater things later on. For example, remember that her Grandfather McKemie had insisted that she study art and music so she could get all "A's" in grade school. She was then able to use that to teach art.

She does the same thing in this chapter. But I don't want to spoil the story . . .

The First Second Night

In the summer of 1951, Davenport was the third largest city in Iowa with a population of over 100,000. Iowa, which had been an agrarian state, had by this time more people in the cities than on the farm. Jim signed a three-year contract and started work immediately. During the summer, administrators have to hire new teachers, sign contracts with current staff, handle class and bus schedules, and repair and upgrade buildings, all of which were Jim's responsibility.

I considered being a stay-at-home wife and mother, but I guess I had been indoctrinated by the McKemie work ethic. In previous years,

Grandfather ranted and raved against relief and Roosevelt's make work programs. He felt America's laborers would be ruined forever. Although Southern Illinois had over fifty percent of able bodied men unemployed, he had trouble getting workers for the farm. They would rather draw relief payments.

As soon as I'd set up our house I started looking for a job. I soon found out that Moline Illinois State College needed a dramatics instructor.

With my Illinois Better Speaker certificate and several newspaper articles about my speaking engagements as references, I was able to get the appointment. Moline, Illinois, though slightly smaller than Davenport, enjoyed a sister city relationship.

Though separated by the wide Mississippi River the two towns shared much in common. A network of bridges made it possible for family members to live and work in both of the towns. Jim and I had bought an "ecology" home, a Molette experimental house in Moline, though we kept our lease on the apartment in Davenport near the administration offices.

My classes were small, but the students were devoted to their art.

They formed the nucleus of the Dramatics Club, which helped with activities like Christmas programs, art festivals, and programs for visiting dignitaries. I convinced the administration and the English department to list two of my classes in Public Speaking and Presentation under their program. I argued that all students should be able to discuss their subject correctly and convincingly.

During my interview, the Dean had stressed the importance of the annual mid-year dramatics production. He also expressed disappointment in the small attendance and lack of support from the community at large.

After my classes and curriculum were more or less settled, I began to think about the major production, or better yet a showcase for the drama department. I studied the plays that had been put on for the past years. There were modern language Shakespeare, Willa Cather plays, dictations of Broadway hits, and plays written specifically for drama productions.

Typically they called for a cast of six or seven characters. Reports were that they were well done, but the audience was usually made up of the relatives and friends of the characters, plus staff members whose attendance was more or less mandatory.

So I decided to write the play and have as many characters involved as possible. Remembering the excitement of talent shows when I first went to the university, I decided to write the play around try outs for induction in the Talent Show.

We put out the casting calls for any type of talent including singing, dancing, comedy skits, recitations, or anything the students' imagination could come up with. Soon, there was a cast of forty. That meant eighty parents, 160 grandparents, and myriad aunts, uncles, friends, as well as just curious people.

The English classes wrote the cover story for the newspaper as a class project. Some of the students in the Drama Club were cast as directors and were scattered strategically throughout the audience to call out suggestions and comments about the actors on stage. This caused some consternation among the audience when they heard someone sitting next to them with a microphone becoming part of the cast.

Unfortunately, some students took my class because it was easier, they thought, then Algebra or Latin. After several sessions of learning the fine art of persuasion, they became enthusiastic ticket sellers and had a ready excuse for prowling the campus and downtown mails and hangouts.

The play was a success and played to a full house. The Dean was very pleased and offered congratulations to everyone.

More Drama

During the summer, I visited a charter school in Chicago. The students, tuition paid, were selected on their abilities in the performing arts.

They then became the performers in the city's many cultural events. Viola! I had the idea for next year's production. I wrote an operetta loosely based on "No! No! Nanette." The play was divided into small shots, depicting a class room situation so that different people would do their own interpretation of how the scene should be played. I recruited about 100 students, many of them from my larger, more enthusiastic drama classes.

A noted dance instructor volunteered to coach the chorus line. The music department supervised the singers; the home economics department made the sets and printed the tickets. The economics and mathematics departments agreed to handle ticket sales and bank the proceeds. The English department turned out reams of copy for newspapers, radio, and TV.

After the show, the Dean told us that for two months before the production, the whole college was involved in some way.

Advanced ticket sales indicated we would need more than one night of production. Soon new tickets were printed up for a second night. This was the first time a second night was needed for a Dramatics Department Show.

On that 2nd night the police department was called for traffic control.

I even heard that some wiseacres from the Economics Department were scalping tickets. The drama department from Davenport also sent a bus load.

After the production, the mayor presented corsages, donated by two florists, to the main actresses. The president of the school board came on a first ever second night production. Needless to say, the college administration was very pleased and that led to the next big change in my life's journey.

Honored

Unbeknownst to me, The Ford Foundation had for some years sponsored a program to find and honor "the best teacher for the year" from the state of Illinois. The Dean, with approval from the administration, nominated me for consideration. In June, I received a wonderful birthday present: I was named Illinois Best Teacher! In addition to the honor, there was a very nice monetary reward that Jim and I decided should be used to get my doctorate.

What a wonderful school year! And what a great way to end it—and I owe it all to my grandfather, who was determined to see me excel in art and speaking when I was a young girl.

CHAPTER 10

Nana has repeatedly said she felt very blessed to have been in the right place at the right time. If she had been able to get a job in Davenport, if she hadn't crossed the Mississippi and taken a job as a Dramatics Director, if the Ford Foundation hadn't picked her as the "Illinois Best Teacher," and a hundred other ifs, this next step in her life's journey might never have happened. Knowing her, though, I would bet she would have found some other way to get her Doctorate in Business Finance. As I heard this next tape, I was amazed again. If any woman could be called Super Woman, it was she.

It All Came Together

With the Ford Foundation Fellowship in hand, the world was my oyster. I could work on my doctorate anywhere. Some noted universities were considered—Wharton School at the University of Pennsylvania, Germany's Heidelberg University home of many noted economists—and our dream state of California with its renowned Stanford. But family considerations prevailed. Jim had one more year on his contract with Davenport, and our daughter, Pat, needed to be within easy commute of family in Illinois. So in the summer of 1953, I made an exploratory trip to the University of Illinois. After all, I had received my Master's Degree there and had a good reputation with the school.

After interviewing, I quickly learned that the School of Business would accept me for their doctorate program. I also found out that a Professor of Sociology was leaving on her sabbatical and needed a house sitter. She had a large, classic home near the university in Urbana. The home had a complete living quarter on the first floor and four large bedrooms plus a study and library upstairs, which she rented to students. After much discussion, we took over her downstairs living quarters, and I became house mother to four students with their myriad problems.

I also found out that the Economics Department needed an instructor for the Economics 101 class. It was taught in one of the big lecture halls (100 or more capacity) on Monday, Wednesday, and Friday at 9 a.m. After an interview I was hired. I was now a faculty member. A lowly instructor yes, but it provided me with a faculty office and a certain prestige when I negotiated with professors in my doctorate program. Almost as by a miracle it had all come together, as if it were meant to be.

Doubling Up

Back in Moline we sold our home. Jim moved back to the apartment in Davenport, and Pat and I moved to Urbana to begin the academic year. Pat was enrolled in the 3rd grade at the University Academy and suddenly acquired four older sisters who spoiled her beyond belief, while I acquired four babysitters, I mean child-sitters. Now all was in readiness.

At the University of Illinois, the doctoral program normally took three years to complete. The first year was a language plus classes, the second year was a second language, plus classes. The final year was used to write a dissertation and pass the "orals" before a faculty committee.

Again, I was under time constraints; I had just one year in the professor's house and one year of funding from the Ford Foundation. The class work I felt sure I could handle, but the competency in two languages was of concern. I decided to enroll in the French department to learn French in September. The four years of high school Latin finally paid off because the root words and sentence structure were the same.

The first exam was in late October and I decided to take it, which no one thought I could pass, including me, but it would be good practice.

Unbelievably, I passed!

Then I made an appeal to the German professor for enrollment in his class, even though the semester was half over. He agreed to help me catch up with the class work I had missed. I crammed like mad until I caught up, and then he said to go ahead on my own because I was already ahead of the class.

The first German exam was in January. With fingers crossed and knowing I could try it again in June, I took and passed the German proficiency exam. It made something of a sensation in the doctorate program because I was now two years ahead of schedule!

My next step was to double up on two years of class work. With both languages out of the way, this wasn't too difficult. I enjoyed teaching Economics 101 and I must have done well because I was offered a contract for the 2nd year.

Throughout my school work and working at school, I still had to spend time as a house-mother to the four student roomers. I had to settle disputes, hurt feelings, boy problems, and money problems amongst the many "crises" that young girls face. All in all, though, I was able to fit everything into my week, but there were many times when I wondered how I was going to do it.

In the last part of the first year of the doctoral program, I began thinking about the requirements for a dissertation. Webster defines a dissertation as a "formal and lengthy discourse in writing: a treatise; a thesis."

It needed to be something that added to the knowledge in your chosen field of study. Everything I thought about had already been researched and published.

I was desperate for thesis ideas when I was called to the dissertation proctor's office. Once again God smiled upon me. The legislature for the State of Illinois had to change the "blue sky laws." Every company that wanted to sell their stocks or bonds had to comply with the state laws, and they were badly outdated. They contacted the business department searching for a professor who would research all the records, find out what was good and what was bad, and make recommendations for the new law. The proctor asked if I would like to take that project as my dissertation. Would I? Wow! I could have kissed him. Instead I went to church next Sunday and thanked God for letting such a plum fall in my lap.

Since I would be doing most of the work in Springfield, the capital of the State, I started looking for a job somewhere between the university and Springfield.

A Side Trip

I had some funds left over from the Ford grant so I grabbed the opportunity to plan a trip to Heidelberg, Germany. I wanted to visit the famous university where so many scholars lived and wrote their economics books. I enrolled in a six-week class in Economics History. With some trepidation, I took my first overseas trip. It was there that I experienced gender discrimination. The students (men) considered me an oddity that had somehow gotten into their midst; women did not belong because business and finance was a man's field.

CHAPTER 11

My grandparents were on the move again. This time it was to Decatur, Illinois, a town of 65,000 located equal-distances from the University of Illinois at Champaign-Urbana and Springfield, the state capital, and where much of Nana's doctoral work could be done. Decatur was the soybean capital of the world and also the home of Millikin University, a small private and exclusive university that was proud of its scholastic reputation, boasting of more Guggenheims, more Oxfordians, and more national honors than any other university outside of the Ivy League colleges back east.

This box containing tapes, articles, and pictures covered this period in Nana's life. Among them were pictures of this very distinguished campus with its ivy covered brick buildings. There were several pictures of my grandparents in formal dress at teas, receptions, proms, etc. They must have traveled everywhere. Another picture showed Nana pointing to a sign which read, "The University of Chili, at Santiago." This must indeed have been an enjoyable time in their lives.

Time pressure was always, it seems, a known factor in Nana's life.

Millikin University was concerned that she earn her doctorate quickly. In looking at a letter dated March 22, 1955, written by the Chairman of the School of Business at the University of Illinois, he was responding to a letter from the Dean at Millikin University, who was asking about Nana's chances of completing her doctorate that year. The Chairman answered positively and added, "All of us here have a great respect and admiration for Mrs. Belt and her extraordinary industriousness. I don't think I have ever seen a person who had greater drive to complete a task before them than she has."

The Blue Sky Laws & the Make or Break Orals

We made ready to move again. I believe we must have been among the first Yuppies (Young Upward-Moving People). Since I could write my dissertation away from campus and Jim didn't renew his contract with Davenport, we could unite the family again. I needed to be within easy commute to the university and Springfield. We looked for a place somewhere in between. We found it in Decatur, a thriving, growing community with a college. Millikin University was a private, expensive, scholastically renowned university with a dream campus. It was located on the major highway between my two required destinations. After research, I learned there was a position open in the Accounting Department in the School of Business. I quickly dusted off and reviewed the course work for a C.P.A. (Certified Public Accountant). Remember that I had taken this by correspondence in the two months before and one year after my pregnancy. Now it might come to my advantage.

With fingers crossed and a prayer on my lips, I applied. Fortunately I was hired, even though I was a woman (all the rest of the professors were male) and I didn't have my doctorate yet (all the rest were Doctors). It was understood that I would finish the work for my Doctor of Philosophy and Business as soon as possible. In addition to doing the research and writing the dissertation, I would be teaching accounting—an area of expertise where I very much feared that my super-achiever students knew more about than I. Oh well, pressure can be turned into a driving force and challenges turned into opportunities. In spite of my very strong fear that I was taking on too much stress and too many challenges, I decided to do it.

During the summer of 1954, we moved into a large, two-story home on Faculty Row across from the football field. Realizing we were going to need help, Jim contacted the principal at Shawnee town. He was seeking a scholastically orientated, but financially-disadvantaged high school graduate, who would welcome the chance to come and live with us and go to college.

Thus Joyce joined us. She was a tall, willowy blond who looked more like our daughter than I did. She stayed with us for several years, obtained her degree, and went back to Shawneetown to teach.

Jim decided to try a new career, real estate sales and development.

With a play on his name, Jim called his firm, "The Gem Realty." Jim joined all the right clubs, Chamber of Commerce, Board of Realtors, Mason, Better Business Bureau, and Rotarians. He took and passed the Illinois real estate exam. Later on, he passed the insurance exam and thus insured our own lives and real estate. Since he was a natural born-trader he put together several lucrative deals. Then if an unusually good deal was listed, he bought it.

For example, we owned and he operated a residential hotel in downtown Decatur opposite the Hilton. He also bought the beautiful home we lived in for the four-to-five years of our stay in Decatur. I soon began to do most of the due-diligence accounting for properties he listed for sale. We made a rather good team.

One time Jim bought a stand-alone restaurant, then he resold it and took a down payment. Unfortunately, the buyers failed within the first year. He sold that restaurant four times, and the down payments we called our summer traveling money. He finally sold to a Korean family and they succeeded, which ended our extra income.

Jim had begun to trade in mobile homes and we often traveled in a motor home he hadn't sold yet. We loved to travel and visited every state, all the Canadian Provinces, and several South American countries but Maine and New Hampshire.

Pat's birthday was in August and we were nearly always on a trip traveling. One year she complained that she'd never had a birthday party. We stayed home that summer so she could have a party.

With the family affairs under control, I could turn my attention toward my two pressing problems. Problem 1: How to teach accounting to students who probably know more about it than I did. Problem 2: How to research and write my dissertation so that I could graduate with the class of 1957. After studying the preregistration rosters for my classes and learning that an economics professor was not only willing, but wanted to continue to teach Accounting 101, I decided to structure my classes on the application of accounting principles, i.e., family budgeting, portfolio analyses, taxation, public accounting, business finance, and cost accounting.

I visited the owners of most of the accounting firms and C.P.A.'s in Decatur and I got their evaluations of our graduates. In addition most agreed to lecture my classes. I then presented my plans to the Dean and he approved this novel approach to teaching accounting. Whew!

I next went to Springfield and met Mr. Robert Roberts, the Undersecretary of Commerce. He was in charge of guiding the passage of the Securities Act of 1955 (Blue Sky legislation) through the Illinois Legislature. The original Securities Act was passed in 1917 and economic conditions had changed in the years since then. Every company that wanted to sell securities in the state of Illinois had to register under this outdated legislation.

Mr. Robert Roberts knew exactly the type of information needed in order to draft the new law.

It would require hours of research and collation of past experience under the old law. It would also require an extensive questionnaire to gauge the current attitude of businessmen toward blue sky laws.

After securing Mr. Roberts' approval of my basic plan of research, I went to the University of Illinois and consulted with the dissertation proctor. He made some basic revisions to make it more scholarly and gave his stamp of approval. Once again, I was thankful for being selected to do this project for my dissertation.

With my two major problems somewhat solved, I could see the light at the end of the tunnel. I was ready to start the new semester in September 1954 at a new (to me) and exciting university. Gradually, ultra-busy activity settled into a doable routine. I taught the three classes and held office hours on Monday, Wednesday, and Friday at Millikin University. On Tuesday, Thursdays, and weekends, I traveled between the Capital and the University of Illinois to do research and collate the results.

The next big job was to prepare a questionnaire to be sent to corporations that had recently or were planning to register securities for sale in the state of Illinois. With the input from personnel from the Department of Commerce, we devised a questionnaire we hoped would help the legislature when they enacted the new securities act. Graduate students reported that a 10 to 20 percent response was normal. However, since my questionnaire went out on Department of Commerce letterhead, the response was 85 percent. Finally the dissertation was finished and the final step, the Orals, were scheduled for late May.

The Orals are a very formal, exacting traditional ritual at the University of Illinois. It's held in an elegant board room and all of the examining professors wear full regalia—caps and gowns and hoods. It is very intimidating and the grad candidate is aware that his or her entire professional future is riding on how well the individual answers the questions on their discipline. The State had published my dissertation and a copy was placed at every chair.

After answering several questions, a senior professor that I had never had in class, signaled that he wanted the floor. He picked up the bound, very professional looking dissertation and ponderously read "An Analysis of Illinois Security Regulations Since 1918 and Recommendations for Revision" by Dr. V. McKemie-Belt. He stressed the word "Dr." He harrumphed and said, "Very presumptuous aren't you?" Every one waited with bated-breath for my answer. They knew, as I did, that in the world of academia, the greatest sin was to claim a doctorate when you didn't have one and that one black ball would mean I wouldn't graduate, and I'd probably lose my job at Millikin. Oh, how to answer? I had probably committed the greatest gaffe. Finally, I said, "Sir, you wouldn't want to make a liar of the State of Illinois, would you?" For about two more hours, I answered questions creditably, I believe. But I was really shaken up. I waited outside for about half an hour (it seemed a lifetime). When I was invited back in, I couldn't tell by looking at their faces what the verdict was. The Chairman then said, "Ms. Virginia Belt, this committee will recommend to the Board of Trustees of the University of Illinois (and then he hesitated) that you be granted a degree of Doctor of Philosophy." Whew!

Finally on June 8, 1955, a select few of us walked across the stage and Board members placed the coveted hood with its blue and orange colors around our shoulders. The family who had attended in mass drew a sigh of relief. The charge that my grandfather had placed on them so many years ago—to see that I got my doctorate—was finally honored. After the festivities and the toasts had been given, we returned to Decatur and I prepared for a trip to New York.

As a form of insurance in case I was not rehired at Millikin, I had applied for and been tentatively accepted for a position in business education at Rensselaer Polytec in upper New York state. I needed to go to Rensselaer for an interview and to check out the community. The Dean's secretary and I made the travel arrangements. I was supposed to call the Dean's office from La Guardia airport and get final plans for visiting the campus. Accordingly, I called and the Dean answered and I spoke to him. I could tell something was wrong. He seemed hesitant and confused. Finally, he arranged for me to stay overnight near the airport and he would call the next morning. When the Dean called, he said they could not hire me because they would not hire a woman professor. He apologized and promised reimbursement of my expenses. He said that he had not realized that the highly qualified Dr. V. McKemie-Belt was a woman. I had not intentionally meant to mislead, but had learned very early that the name Virginia was not an asset in my chosen field of business.

I flew back to Decatur with mixed emotions of resentment and relief. There my mood improved because I found an offer of reemployment back at Millikin. Jim had fit into the realty community and enjoyed the challenge of making real estate deals.

Our daughter would be in the second grade and was making friends, especially Ronnie, the boy next door. Joyce, our mother's assistant, was happy in her education classes at the Junior College. With the doctorate secured, I could now concentrate on being the best (better) "Professor at Millikin."

The students came from many states and countries, attracted by the high academic standards. Therefore, Millikin was almost a self-contained community, providing room and board in addition to tuition. The staff focused on social interaction of students and faculty. Thus, faculty were required to attend games, plays, teas, and faculty affairs. Most fraternities and sororities had a chapter on campus. Since Jim and I were the youngest faculty members, we were soon in demand as chaperons at "Greek" affairs. That meant a lot of formal wear for both of us.

We were living in a university owned house located on a street known as "faculty row" running parallel to the football field. In this early September twilight, all were well and accounted for.

Jim and I were quietly rocking back and forth in the white glider on the elongated front porch. Patti was playing a game of Jacks with Ronnie, and Joyce had emerged with the ever-present text book in her hand. As the music from the band practicing at one end of the field was punctuated by shouts from the football team, practicing at the other end of the field, I knew with absolute certainty that all was very right with my world.

CHAPTER 12

It's been a while since I was able to transcribe this next chapter in Nana's memoirs. I have been working on my teaching certificate for the ancient art of Yoga. Although Yoga originated in the Hindu culture of India, many in the Western World have begun to practice it and value the quiet time out in our hectic 24/7 busy world. This next folder in Nana's memoirs says "The Sabbatical Year: Rest, Renewal, and Research." Then in big letters it says, "California here we come!" There are a lot of pictures of scenic places in this folder. Obviously they took advantage of their sabbatical year of rest and relaxation. Let's find out what she did on her quiet time out.

Sabbatical Travels, an Offer & the Loss of a Dream Appointment

Although we were well situated and very content in Decatur, Illinois, the lure of California was still exciting to us. It's like an unconsummated plan or an itch that's never scratched. Twenty years after our first plans to go to California, we decided to try again. Finally, the time seemed right for us to explore the economic and social opportunities in California.

At Millikin University, they offered full-time professors a year off for rest, renewal, and research after a professor had completed seven years. It was a sabbatical or a Sabbath.

After establishing a career, a social life, buying a home, and having more than one person to consider, planning to take a year off presents a lot of complications. However, we decided to accept the challenge. I applied for and was granted my sabbatical. We dusted off all the old plans and identified all the scenic places we wanted to see on the way west.

We could take at least three summer months to travel. We would arrive in California before the academic year started, and we could determine if there was an opportunity for us.

The university paid me my basic salary, but none of the perks. Jim wouldn't be able to do any profitable deals, getting only a small percentage from deals done under his brokerage licenses. Then there would be the expense of travel and living for a year away from home. Fortunately, he had just bought a nice motor home for our travels. So I began looking for a way to make extra money.

The Department of Education was offering a grant to someone who would research the teaching of economics in the high schools of America. Ah, right down my alley! Since we would be traveling across country anyway, we could stop at high schools in the towns we were passing through and I could interview the principals. I applied for the grant, submitted my proposal and won. Viola, there was our traveling money! Later, my report was published by the U. S. Department of Education in a compendium of high school subjects. Our house was rented. Joyce had earned her teaching certificate and returned to Shawneetown to teach. I had arranged with the school district to home school Patty. All was in readiness. California, here we come!

Heading Out

I could write a travelogue about all the places we visited as we crisscrossed the country on our way west. We saw all the must-see places, and some of our most memorable experiences happened in the small towns we visited so that I could interview principals to fulfill the terms of my grant. For example, in a little town in New Mexico, I met a principal in the auditorium who was trying to direct a group of students as they prepared for an important State Honors program. Never knowing when to let well enough alone, and also realizing that I would not get the interview I needed until he had the program down pat, I decided to help. Depending on my experience as a director of drama, I began to make suggestions and before I knew it I was directing the production! We stayed for three days and I had the satisfaction of seeing the students put on a very creditable show. After the show, I received heartfelt thanks and a very comprehensive interview from the principal.

Moving On

We finally crossed into California. We had already decided to head for Orange County on the Pacific coast, one of the fastest growing counties and one of the richest.

The county offered the best chance of finding out whether we would find the "gold" in California. One of the things that surprised us as we traveled through Southern California was the large areas of desert and the sparse population. As we drove closer to the Pacific, the population increased exponentially. It was wall-to-wall people. You could pass through one city to another, and only by looking at the signs could you tell that you were in a different one. We chose to stop at the beautiful city of Buena Park near Disneyland and Knott's Berry Farm for a few days. Jim had lined up an interview, after which he was offered a teaching/administrative position. He would teach while he studied for and got his real estate broker's license. Teaching certificates were transferable from Illinois to California, but the real estate licenses weren't. I also interviewed and was offered a position teaching economics in Santa Ana College. It looked like we were set to stay in this great state.

We headed north for Los Angeles to see all the many things that the big city had to offer in the way of museums, theaters, Hollywood, and UCLA.

During my visit to UCLA, I found out that Mr. Clendenin was the Dean of the School of Business. I had been using his text in Business Finance at Millikin University for several years, and I hoped to meet him. Fortunately, he was in his office working on the 10th revision of his popular text. Thankfully, he was free when I approached his secretary for an appointment. When Dr. Clendenin learned that I had been using his text to teach, he wanted my feedback. I spent the day with him and, at lunch, I explained that we were in California scouting out opportunities. It was a special day for me, and he thanked me for my time as well.

When I arrived back at our prearranged motor home park, a message from UCLA was waiting for me. I was asked to call Dr. Clendenin. The next morning I returned the call, and he offered me a position as associate professor teaching business finance, using his text, of course. I was overwhelmed, overjoyed. A position at UCLA! That exceeded my fondest dreams.

To celebrate my exceedingly good fortune, we decided to really live it up and go to the famous Freemont Hotel for dinner. I was on Cloud-nine . . . then I crashed to earth. We were refused admission to the dining room because we were not properly dressed. Instead, we had our celebratory dinner at McDonald's. (I've since acquired a successful portfolio of McDonald common stock.)

Dashed Hopes

Originally, we had planned to travel north through Oregon and Washington, then during the beautiful fall months we would travel east through Northern United States and Southern Canada. There were so many things to see and to do. Without any definite schedule, we had planned to complete the 6,000 mile trip and be back home for Christmas. Now the plans had to change. Jim called Buena Park District, accepted the position and was told to report as soon as possible. I felt that I had to get back as soon as I could to talk to the Dean at Millikin. I knew that he would not be happy. Sabbaticals were not given to professors so they could look for another job.

We packed up and planned the quickest and shortest route between San Francisco and Decatur. We made the 2,000 mile trip in three days, but it was too late. To my chagrin, the Dean from UCLA called my Dean to confirm that I was a faculty member in good standing. My Dean replied that I was a faculty member now and for some time in the future. In other words, back off. She is not available!

CHAPTER 13

Fate. It is defined as the power that is supposed to determine the outcome of events. Destiny? Prophetic? Having important consequences? Decisive? Controlled as if by fate.

I was searching for a word or phrase that would indicate something that maybe wasn't meant to be. Could it be that my grandparents were not supposed to migrate to California? How else to explain the many times they made plans to go there during the past twenty years. I know they finally made it though, because I was born in California and lived there most of my life. I've also traveled all over the United States in "Little Mimi," their travel trailer. Let's find out how and when that happened.

A Non-Sabbatical Year & the Mermaid

The plum, a professorship at UCLA, was snatched out of my hands.

After a mad dash across the country and a vain attempt to talk to the Dean at Millikin before the Chairman from UCLA could do so, I learned I was too late.

My Dean said that I had to complete another year before I could be released.

Professional courtesy prevailed and the offer of the professorship was withdrawn.

Many new plans now had to be made. Jim had already accepted the position in California, and we had bought a home in Buena Park. Talk about counting your chickens before they hatch! After much discussion and troubleshooting, we decided that we must become a long distance family. Jim would move to California and Patty and I would stay in Illinois.

We had to unravel many of the things we had done slowly and expensively. We bought back our home from the renters, Patty was re-enrolled in her school and had to say hello to the classmates she had said goodbye to while on her way to glamorous California, Disneyland, and Hollywood. I talked to my Dean and learned that he had not signed my replacement yet. If I would give up my Sabbatical, they would love to have me back. So, I said hello again to my surprised colleagues.

The Dean explained he had been struggling with scheduling when UCLA called and said, "We've hired Dr. Belt and wanted to verify that she has been on your faculty for over seven years." He was taken by surprise and felt insulted by the tone of the question. He felt sorry that he had ruined my chances at UCLA. But I really knew that I owed Millikin another year after the granting of a sabbatical. I was just hoping that an exception could be made.

In spite of my disappointment, it was best that things happened as they did. When we left on the sabbatical, we had intended to be gone for only part of the year. If we found that California or the west was where we wanted to settle, we would have had time to settle our affairs in Decatur. It was a very strange year.

There was a feeling of impermanence, a sense of waiting for something to happen. When in committee meetings and the discussion concerned long term plans for the university, I felt that I should not participate because I might not be there to help implement the plans. I did not try for a grant as I had done every year, and I knew the university wanted me to do something that would bring honor to the school.

In all of Jim's letters and calls, he was full of praise about California.

He had visited many places of interest: Knott's Berry Farm, the Wax Museum, the ocean, and Disneyland, just to name a few. He was enjoying his work and was studying for his real estate broker's exam. But what fascinated Pat the most was that Jim was having a pool put in our backyard. It seemed that everyone in California had to have a pool. She wanted to go—now!

During the Christmas vacation, Pat and I flew to California. We discovered that it was everything that Jim had described and more. We were like kids in a candy store trying to cram everything that Southern California had to offer in our two-week vacation.

Much to our daughter's disappointment, the pool was not ready for swimming. It had been plastered and was waiting for the final drying before the water was put in. Pat had spent many an hour drawing pictures until she had become a talented artist. She got the idea of putting a mermaid in the bottom of the pool. She drew a rough outline of one and we bought hundreds of tiles in all shades of blues and greens for a creative solid pattern and hundreds of black tiles for the outline. Pat pressed the tiles into the almost dry plaster and finished a ten-foot long mermaid before we had to leave. When we saw it later after water had been added, the mermaid appeared to shimmer and swim. Our pool became a show place. Word spread and she got offers to do several mermaids.

We were sold!

I now had to see what job opportunities were offered. I learned that California State University at Long Beach, California, had an opening in the finance department. Long Beach was an international port with most of the imports from the Orient coming through there and being stored in massive warehouses that lined the Pacific shoreline for many miles. Smaller coastal vessels, miles and miles of railroads, and a constant stream of big semi-trucks distributed those imports to the rest of the country.

CSU was an enormous university with about 22,000 students. It had a large enrollment of international students, mostly from the Orient. I made an appointment to meet with the Chairman of the Finance

Department, and wow, what a huge campus! It was like a city in itself with restaurants, stores, and massive buildings that covered many square miles. I learned later on that it was the second largest university by enrollment in the United States.

I finally found the faculty dining room for the School of Business. I met with the Chair and some other faculty members. If hired, I would be the first woman in the School of Business and Commerce. After the luncheon, I met with the Dean and was told that he had received favorable reports from those who attended. He had me fill out countless forms that were necessary before I could be hired by the State. From his secretary, I learned that my chances were good for an appointment because I had been asked to fill these out.

Heading Back

Now it was time to go back to central Illinois and Millikin. Our daughter went with some degree of reluctance. Once home, I met with the Dean and submitted my resignation. In addition to our regular work and schooling, my spare time was taken up with plans to move to California permanently. Jim sold his real estate firm to his two employees, and they made their first commissions helping me sell our home and the residential hotel. It was our goal to have everything packed up and ready to move by the end of the school year in June.

The Beltonian was a grand name for our residential hotel. It was the oldest hotel in Decatur, probably built in the 1920s. Big chain hotels had moved into Decatur, so it had been converted to a residential hotel. Its five stories contained a mixture of residents. Some had lived in the hotel before we bought it; others came and went as their finances dictated. We also received the overflow from the Hilton next door.

Two of the hotel tenants are noted here because they influenced us.

The first was Lucy. She operated the restaurant on the first floor. She was about as wide as she was tall and had a fabulous personality. You could hear her booming laugh throughout the lobby. She was a good cook, but a lousy business woman.

One day I went in for lunch and she came to my table and said, "Madam Prof, you tell me something, See, every table is full and look at the people waiting to get in. Now why am I going broke?"

While I was looking over the scene to find an answer, a cook came up to report they were out of potatoes. Lucy reached into her pocket, pulled out a bill and told him to run around the corner to the convenience store and buy ten pounds. Ah-ha, I had part of the answer! Whenever our busy schedules could mesh, we installed an inventory control system, arranged to buy in bulk, and set us a simple income and cost ledger. Things began to improve and Lucy was grateful.

In spite of her great size, Lucy was very popular with the men. Our night clerk reported that she visited the rooms of our male guests rather indiscriminately. One guest was a man named Johnny. He was tall, lanky and weather beaten. They made a strange Mutt and Jeff pair. Johnny was a master carpenter and designer. Tell him what you wanted built and he could visualize it and tell you with great accuracy how many nails, board feet, cement, etc., you would need for the job. However, he would not tell you how soon he would finish, because Johnny was the town drunk. He was also peaceful and friendly when drunk. All the policemen in the downtown district knew Johnny.

They would pick him up, bring him back to the hotel and help the night clerk put him to bed.

When we first moved to Decatur, I'd heard Johnny was an excellent builder. I just didn't realize how good he was. Ever since I had seen the movie "Gone with the Wind," I had longed for a Southern Colonial home like Tara.

The home that Jim and I bought during our second year in Decatur was a two story brick with a small stoop over the front door. I had wondered if we could convert it into a "Tara" with four big white columns over the front of the house.

One day, Jim brought Johnny from the hotel, and I explained what I wanted. He started sketching, and soon had a workable design and the cost involved. It was even better than I had imagined! I was also warned to be patient.

Johnny started work with a vengeance. The stoop was torn out and that made the front door impassable. The forms for the huge cement porch were built and then Johnny disappeared. No one could find him. A week later he appeared for work without any explanation. In spite of this happening several times, it was finished and was worth all the anxiety. He built an extra garage on our house as well.

Then disaster struck!

One night Johnny came into the hotel, fell down a set of stairs and broke his neck. It was then we learned that he came from a rather affluent family when his brother, a lawyer, stormed into town seeking vengeance. We called our lawyer and insurance company. Fortunately nothing was found on the stairs that could have caused his fall. The coroner's inquest showed that he had three times the legal limit of alcohol in his system, and the police testified about his long term use of alcohol.

I believe Lucy probably did the most good. She told about Johnny's friendship with Jim. Whatever or however, Johnny's brother left with his body and we heard nothing more. It had given us a good scare and we were determined to get enough insurance. Is it ever possible to have enough?

Falling into Place

The contract from CSU at Long Beach arrived, and the last slot fell into place. Now it was total commitment. Full steam ahead. I also received a pleasant surprise: an associate professorship. The normal progression is instructor, assistant, associate, and finally full. One is usually old and wizened before reaching full professorship. My new goal was to reach full as soon as possible.

I had been selected to lead the faculty processional for that last year's graduation at Millikin. Carrying the mace is an honor bestowed by the faculty senate made up of senior professors. I felt guilty for leaving a university that had been so good to me.

Graduation was scheduled for Friday, June 4th. Everything had to be arranged on or around that date. The Hotel was sold and after the scare we had, I was glad to see it go. The stately Southern Colonial house, Tara, sold quickly and I arranged for occupancy on June 7th. Keys and final papers were to be left with the Realtors who bought Jim's business. The movers came with boxes and packing materials, and showed us how to pack efficiently. After living in the same place for over seven years we had acquired a lot of "stuff."

The movers were to come on Saturday and begin the long drive cross country.

The man who bought my car was to drive us to the airport, part of the purchase price. Jim would meet us in Los Angeles, and we would drive to our new home and wait for the movers. Pat said she would be swimming and leave the unpacking to us.

Finally, maybe . . . California, here we come!

CHAPTER 14

The declaration "Here we come California" that appeared at the end of so many chapters in my Nana's life story can now be changed to read, "California, here we are." Nana and my mom arrived at LAX airport on June 6th, my Nana's 39th birthday. She says she is going to be 39+ forever. She was so young when she started teaching, she always added a year to her actual age. Now, in some strange "nanology" kind of math, she says she can now subtract a year or two each year and thus, she equals it out and stays thirty-nine for the next forty years. Go figure, but that's Nana!

California at Last–Oogie & the Exploding Beer Bottles

It was a unanimous decision. For this summer, all thoughts of business, career advancement, and promotions were to be put on the back burner. It was time for family reunion, for enjoying our new home, neighborhood, and all the wonders that California offered. With so many choices of things we wanted to do, our biggest problem was to prioritize.

After much family discussion, we decided to spend the first month at home. We wanted to enjoy our new swimming pool, getting to know our neighbors, visiting the many attractions like Disneyland and Knott's Berry Farm's "Famous Chicken Dinners on Sunday." And we wanted to spend time decorating our home. Our daughter, Pat, got a Siamese kitten and she decided to decorate her room in its colors: chocolate and champagne. We found a spread and pillow shams with

Siamese cat patterns. She painted a "slinky" Siamese on one wall, and with a lot of ceramic Siamese scattered all over, creating a picture-purrrfect room.

After we had been there a few days, Jim took us around to meet the neighbors. We lived on a circle with five homes. I was determined to be neighborly this time. I remembered that, in spite of the six years we lived in our beautiful colonial home, I only had a nodding acquaintance with our neighbors in Decatur due to the business of life.

Before long we had arranged cook-outs, swimming parties, shopping trips, and trips to must-see places. In spite of often thinking that I wanted to study and get my CFA designation (Certified Financial Analyst), I pushed it to the back of my mind and had fun. Toward the end of June, we began studying maps and scenic routes to find the best roads that would take us to the most places that we wanted to see.

We decided that we wanted to swim in the Pacific Ocean, so we headed for the southern coast of Orange County. We especially liked Huntington Harbour, an ocean front enclave of beautiful homes just south of Long Beach where I was going to be teaching. Outside of Huntington Harbour and heading south along the coast toward Newport Beach was a State Park with facilities for swimming and water sports. We spent three days in that area and in spite of the fact that it appeared to be overcast, we all got sunburned.

We decided to take a quick trip home to Buena Park and when we arrived we found an extremely large, gray, male cat in our backyard. No one in the neighborhood knew of its origins. Jim put it out front, thinking it might go home. It didn't. The animal shelter reported no lost gray cat. So this huge cat adopted *us*. Talk about a case of arrested development! Given a chance, he would crawl into any of our laps and try to suck on an ear. He was also a very timid cat, afraid of his own shadow. We put a big dish of food outside for him. Even though he was many times bigger than our tiny Siamese kitten, she would drive him away from his dish of food. He would only eat if the little kitten was nowhere in sight.

On the Road Again

Leaving Los Angeles, we opted to take the coastal northern route of 101. It was the most scenic, but it was the slowest. Because of its winding, meandering lanes, one was lucky to travel thirty miles per hour. I especially liked Santa Barbara, a historic college town. When we reached Big Sur, we felt as if we had died and gone to heaven. Pat and I spent a lot of time sketching some beautiful wind blown and mis-shaped trees of the coastal scenes. Pat loved to sketch these trees. Further up the coast, we enjoyed the sites of San Francisco, with its majestic Golden Gate Bridge, its historical 1851 fire and the earthquakes, and the most numerous fish eateries.

We wanted to complete the northern half of the scenic route to the Oregon border. By the time we reached Eureka, we had seen all the coast line we could absorb. We cut across to Route 5, which ran straight and true down the middle of the state. It was fast, boring, and *hot*.

Running alongside of the major highway was the large, open canal bringing southern California's drinking water supply. I thought how easy it would be for bio-terrorists to poison it. I remembered an incident that had frightened me. Our friend had a large tank full of many types of exotic fish. A pail had been used with a small amount of poison for spraying on roses to kill aphids. The pail was rinsed out and left to dry in the sun. About a month later, the maid had used that pail to add water to the tank. The next morning, all the fish were floating at the top of the tank—dead.

Sweet Sixteen

We had a good reason for wanting to get home as soon as possible.

August 6th was Pat's birthday. She would be sweet sixteen and eligible for a driver's license. We had bought her a small, lime green, car. It was a used French Citron. Pat was delighted.

We finally pulled into our driveway on August 2nd. There was time to wash clothes and when everything was dried, we took long hot showers, and went for a swim. Home cooked meals tasted good even though I've never claimed to be a good cook. We got reacquainted with the cats, which seemed to be no worse because of our absence.

Jim checked the former owner's wife and found that Pat's car was ready. The big day arrived and she was surprised and delighted when Jim drove that tiny green car up with the big red ribbon that said, *Happy Birthday!*

Patty called the car "*Oogie*" (because of the oogie sound that the horn made) and Jim spent much of the next week teaching her to drive. We found out later that she had been sneaking the family car out for careful midnight drives around our block for years.

All too soon the reality of work set in and it was time to get ready for my new position. The last couple of weeks before September flew by for all of us. We could no longer continue to live in our bathing suits. The clothing that had been right for Illinois did not work in the mild climate of California.

California styles were far more relaxed than Mid-western. The times when I went out dressed with hat, nylons, gloves, and heels, I was asked if I were going to a funeral. Brand new outfits were a necessity.

I also spent some time in the libraries gathering material I wanted to share with my class. We got Pat enrolled in the high school and purchased school books and supplies. Jim began looking into the material he would need to know to pass the California Realtor's exam. He also wanted to get his insurance license so he could sell the insurance when he sold the property.

A Drunken Cat

One Saturday night we were awakened by a sound of "popping." On and off for about an hour this rather loud sound of popping corks and glass breaking disturbed our sleep. Jim got up to try to find the source of the disturbance. When he came back into the room smiling, he told me to get dressed: I had to see it to believe it.

The neighbor's garage, which was next to our bedroom, was a mini still. He had rows and rows of beer, bottled and corked, filling his garage. Jack was a nice fellow, but you never saw him without a bottle of beer in his hand.

Now he had beer leaking out from under his garage door and running into the street. The next day the entire area still smelled of beer! We were sitting in the backyard laughing over the exploding beer when the big gray cat came bounding over the backyard fence and "staggered "over to his food dish. The little Siamese kitten came up, expecting Gray Boy to give way like he always did. Well, this time he growled at her. She backed up with an expression that seemed to say, "What got into him?" Beer, Fifi, beer.

Excerpts from letters, newspapers, magazines, and professional journals collected by the staff of Ralph Edward's "This is Your Life" in 1954 for her appearance on the show.

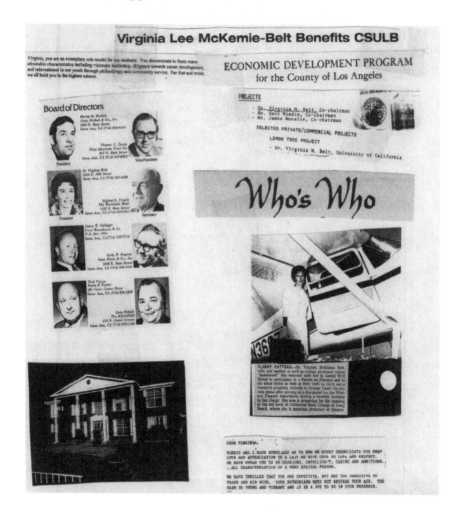

Dr. McKemie-Belt is an owner or staff member of a number of educational institutions supplying specialized training under government contracts or teaching business administration on the university level. Projects range from teaching the art of self-employment to unemployed scientists and engineers to teaching job skills to the mentally handicapped.

V. McKemie-Belt, Ph.D.
Executive Vice President

) years financial and
lucational experience.
icturer and author –
pital markets and
isiness finance.

S. Business Finance	University of Illinois
.D. – Financial Management	University of Illinois
onors – Phi Beta Kappa, Phi Kappa Phi, Artus	
63 - 71 Professor	Graduate Faculty, CSC-LB
Lecturer	UCI, Insurance Institute
Consultant	SBA, HRD, Econ. Educ. C.
President	Financial Programming
Sec./Treas.	New Age Schools

From the desk of –

B. W. KETTENHOFEN

Dr. Belt,

As an educator at the college and university level, I knew your textbook would undoubtedly meet several criteria and I want to add an unusual one to your portfolio! After many years of industry experience, I continued/decided to attempt a graduate degree of a far better to do so on many counts. Your class is my first undertaking and I can sincerely state that I have been continually stimulated to the point where I definitely plan to complete the requirements for an MBA degree. In addition, my wife and I are most gratified to know that there is a politically conservative educator shaping our young people – you are to be commended! Best of luck at C.S.C.

Sincerely,
B. W. Kettenhofen

(over)

FINANCIAL RESOURCES

Dr. McKemie-Belt, as president of Financial Planning and Programming, is active in the capital financing field. After years of experience as financial consultant to business, investment banking firms, and government agencies, her contacts and expertise make it possible for TRI to supply personnel and services in the critical financial areas. While serving as officer and member of the board of Western Finance Association, Dr. McKemie-Belt became aware of the financial acumen of most professors, trustees, and finance advisors in the western states and can call on their services when needed.

The aim of TRI is to bring an uniquely tight system of financial management to business firms.

Dr. Virginia McKemie Belt Named to Education Council

Mr. and Mrs. Charlie McKemie, south of Benton, have been notified of the appointment of their daughter, Dr. Virginia McKemie Belt, to the President's Council for Economic Education. The major objective of the council is the dissemination of economic truth and analysis of the economic currency...

V. McKemie-Belt, Ph.D.
Executive Vice President

20 years financial and
educational experience.
Lecturer and author –
capital markets and
business finance.

B.S. Business Finance — University of Illinois
Ph.D. – Financial Management — University of Illinois
Honors – Phi Beta Kappa, Phi Kappa Phi, Artus
1963 - 71 Professor — Graduate Faculty, CSC-LB
Lecturer — UCI, Insurance Institute
Consultant — SBA, HRD, Econ. Educ. C.
President — Financial Programming
Sec./Treas. — New Age Schools

Sixth Edition

1970-71

Former students who took Dr. Virginia Lee McKemie-Belt's courses in investment, capital formation and business finance remember her fondly as an instructor of rare liveliness and wit.

CBA alumnus Steven Besbeck, President of Creative Computer Applications, Inc., for example, recalls equally her enthusiasm and her humorous anecdotes. "She was clearly one of the best professors I had," he says.

Just a little note, Merle is our third boy to take
Algebria C J H S. Thought I had heard all remarks
ooy could make in regard to his teacher until
one eve he said,(I bet we got the best Algebria
Teacher in the whole school or anyplace for
that matter.)

Well just wanted to share the remark with you.

Sincerly

Mrs. Emmett Dunn

All of us here have great respect and admiration for Mrs.
Belt and her extraordinary industriousness. I don't think I have
ever seen a person who had greater drive to complete the task before
him than she has. I hope that she is making a good impression at
Millikin and that she will continue to have good progress.

Sincerely yours,

H K Allen

H. K. Allen
Chairman

COLLEGE OF COMMERCE & BUSINESS ADMINISTRATION

UNIVERSITY OF ILLINOIS · URBANA, ILLINOIS

Dear Mrs. Belt:

May I express my congratulations for the
outstanding success you enjoyed for the '51
Revue. The quality of the play was good and
the quality of the acting was outstanding.
I think that you should be very happy with
the realization that for the first time in
our history you over sold the house by
several hundred people. I wish for your
continued success and happiness in your work.

Very sincerely yours,

Walter H. Congdon, Prin.

STOCK   AND   SHARE   BROKERS
MEMBERS OF THE STOCK EXCHANGE OF MELBOURNE

Dear Virginia,

Thought you might be interested in joining a panel to study
the economics of alternative energy sources thru agribusiness
sponsored by the UN. Your recent work on the jojoba and your
long association as a lecturer with the United Nations makes
you eminently suitable. You're the only Yank I know whose
interest in our Area might induce you to "stand the charge"

I would like a copy also for my personal file. Your
attention to this matter would be most gratefully appreciated. Please give my personal regards to Doctor
Belt who I feel is one of the most competent instructors
I have ever encountered.

Sincerely,

LtCol. E.R. Rogal, USMC.   *Edward Roy Rogal*
5651 Emile Street
Omaha 6, Nebraska
16 February, 1963

CALIFORNIA STATE UNIVERSITY
LONG BEACH

OFFICE OF THE PRESIDENT

January 2, 1974

Dear Virginia:

I was delighted to read the article on you which appeared
in the November 18th Santa Ana Register when it came in through the
clipping service. You have received more coverage from the Register than
all of the press releases of the University for the past year, and that story
has more value to the University than most of the press releases for the past
year. Congratulations. I have enjoyed reading it and have enclosed
the copy in case you have need of an extra.

The Citizens National Bank

Dear Dr. Belt:

Because George Champion, of the Chase Manhattan Bank, made
such a complimentary remark about you in a letter that I received today, I thought you might like to see a copy of the letter,
so I am enclosing it. I might add that I concur fully with George
Champion's opinion.

CHAPTER 15

Many of the previous chapters ended with "California here we come!"

My Grandparents' long-time dream of making it out to the west coast finally materialized after much effort and twenty years. My Nana's career had her traveling all over the world on speaking engagements and tours for the American Bankers Association and the United Nations, but her professorship at California State University would be her home base for the next twenty-five years.

This move laid the ground work for me to be born and raised in Huntington Beach, California; a town that would later provide me with an abundant, safe, and magical childhood; a town who's police cars had logos on them that actually stated it to be "The safest city in the world" back in the 70s and 80s.

The Next 25 Years

Little did I know that as I walked through the doors of the School of the Business and Commerce on the campus of California State University (CSU) in Southern California that this would be my base of operation for the next twenty-five years. Upon entering the first building, I faced a series of glass cubicles with an identification sign above and a clerk behind each cubicle. There were a few students in front of each area. They, like myself, were probably trying to get a jump on the mass of students who would be standing in lines behind signs marked *registered, unregistered, schedule change, cashier, student loans, advisors* in the various disciplines, and more. I spotted a sign reading "staff" and decided to head that way.

After identifying myself, I explained that I wanted a tour of the building before the start of classes the next week. The clerk introduced me to Jane, who worked in public relations in the Dean's office. That was a fortuitous meeting because Jane also edited the school newspaper. She would become my best public relations advocate. For many years my future activities were reported on a regular basis.

While touring the campus I told Jane I'd noticed the prominence of the term "The Forty-Niners." Forty-Niner Student Center, Forty-Niner Bookstore, football team, streets, and even a newspaper called the Forty-Niner. She explained that the original Board of Trustees wanted something that would separate this new campus from all the other universities in California.

Someone pointed out that the Gold Rush of '49 had started the big migration to California, Aha! A good name for a university that was to become one of the largest in the nation measured by enrollment.

The School of Business, like many others on campus, was a long, rectangular, three-story building. It was very utilitarian; no ivy covered brick walls. Behind the entrance cubicles was the office of the Dean of the School and his many secretaries and assistants. All summer long, they had been preparing course descriptions and catalogs to help the students and advisors chose the curriculum that would eventually lead to a degree. They had been scheduling too few classrooms for too many students. Classrooms were usually filled from 7 a.m. until 10 p.m. five days a week and often on Saturdays. To cater to academic egos, they had to juggle too few offices between too many staff members. What a nightmare!

Surrounding the Dean's office were smaller offices for the chairmen of the different disciplines, i.e., accounting, business administration, computer science, finance, labor relations and marketing. Behind the business offices was a long, narrow room facing the quad, its green grass and lovely flower beds providing color to relieve the general drabness of the decor. This room provided a place for students to wait and study or socialize between classes.

Coca-Cola and other vendors provided snacks, mostly unhealthy, for the waiting students. At one end of the room were racks with newspapers and audience specific journals and periodicals.

Jane explained that the second floor consisted of assigned-according-to-rank faculty offices, as were the parking spaces. At both ends of the floor were large offices, comparable in space and location to the large, 100-student classrooms that we saw on the first floor. Those rooms had rows and rows of standard size desks with two chairs per desk, one behind the desk for the faculty member and one beside the desk for the student seeking teacher advice or consultation. Since the desks were in such close proximity, I wondered how much meaningful consultation took place.

Instructors shared office space and, therefore, carried their office with them. Instructors were first-year graduates with MBAs or PHBs without teaching experience. Other instructors were specialists like lawyers, CPAs, CEOs, CFOs, and governmental types who were willing to share their knowledge with us. Whenever possible, I sat in on these classes in order to keep abreast of the many law changes that occurred in our field.

Assistant professors also shared these large rooms, however, they had exclusive use of their assigned space for the semester. You could spot an assistant's desk because of the brass nameplate on the desk. Professors take these brass nameplates with them as they advance in rank and even into retirement. Assistants are usually teachers with prior experience or sometimes a new hire with an outstanding academic record.

Between the four large offices at each end of the floor was a long, wide corridor with polished wooden floors. On either side of the corridor were identical doors with a number and a small nameplate with a name or names on it. *Full* professors occupied a room by themselves, thus only one name on the door.

A New Home

I came in as an associate, hence, two names on Door 222. Jane opened the door and I saw two desks, four chairs, and two bookcases. The desk nearest the door was covered with opened books and papers. The bookcase was filled with books on finance. The name plate read "Dr. Mark Reis." The top of my desk and the bookcase were void of all signs of habitation, but on the desk in its isolated splendor was a brass nameplate "Dr. V. McKemie-Belt." This would be my new home.

The third floor had the smaller classrooms for advanced classes and specialty lectures. On one end of the corridor was a lab room with many types of business machines and very crude, early computers. Classes were scheduled there, but the room and use of the machines was available to all students and faculty. Over the years, and as the computer models improved, many of us became computer savvy in that room.

The building had no elevators, and as Jayne and I walked down to the first floor, I realized that I must make some changes, especially in my shoe style. The relaxed and gracious pace of Millikin University had spoiled me.

Now I must get up and go if I am to keep up with the hurried and harried life style of the Californians. California here I am, now go, go, go!

CHAPTER 16

I remember registration to be one of the most maddening, frustrating, and aggravating experiences; hundreds of students scurrying about, everyone full of anxiety, confusion and panic, all trying desperately to navigate around so many obstacles in order to obtain their coveted degrees. I always felt that you needed to take a whole semester class just on going to school in order to learn how to effectively navigate through college.

When you were unable to get into your intended course, you faced a whole slew of subsequent fiascoes. It was just this type of scheduling fiasco that led my Nana to switch from a history major to her fortuitous degree in finance. After much moving about, my grandparents finally settled down in California and for the next twenty-five years Nana made room #222 at CSU uniquely her own.

Registration & Room 222

Although I had not been assigned any duties for registration day, I decided to go on campus anyway. It was the beginning of my new job and I was anxious to get started. I'd loaded my car with books and lecture notes; I wanted to make my room look lived in and put my mark on it.

As I expected, the campus was in full swing with the parking lot filled and the sidewalks jammed. The entry to the building, which was nearly deserted last week, was now wall-to-wall people. Long lines were behind every cubicle.

Tables manned by faculty members, usually instructors, were there to assist students planning their schedule of classwork for the semester. Students with dog-eared catalogs listing all classes offered and a class schedule, which they struggled to fill in, stood in frustration waiting to talk to an advisor. Long ago memories of my struggles to get the classes I wanted and needed made me empathize with a frustrated student who yelled, "But I have to take that class!"

There were general education classes that everyone has to take, as well as classes to meet the requirements for a major and a minor. There were also electives. Often, a lab class would take a block of time that conflicted with the only time a required major class was scheduled. Something had to give.

A university on a semester plan like CSU charged tuition for sixteen units, whether the student could find these classes or not. Often he would take any class that would fit into an empty slot of unused time. Sometimes that can have unexpected results. In my case, I took a Money and Banking class and fell in love with business.

A Friend and Proctor

I went hunting for Dr. Reis and found him in the little office behind the Dean's office. These offices were occupied by the appointed chairmen of the different departments, such as Finance. Dr. Reis was, I would guess, in his late 50s or early 60s. He had a very athletic build and fit his clothes perfectly.

But on this day his tie was loosened and his hair rumpled, as if he had been running his hand through it. He had sent me an introductory packet that contained a schedule of the classes I would teach this semester. However, an attached note said it was subject to change. I hoped to get a final schedule and check the library for a reading list.

My final schedule was three hours of Investments 101, three hours of Financial Management, and three hours of Investment Analysis. An associate professor taught nine hours per week with three hours of office for student consultation, exams and preparation for the next class. Not a normal forty hour work week, that's for sure! I was delighted to learn that we used Dr. Clendin's text in Principles of Investments 101.

If the students had trouble devising a class schedule, the deans and chairmen had double trouble. They had to offer as many classes as space, time, and professors would allow. Then they had to deal with the professors. What a group of prima donnas! They were always sensitive to any disrespect to their rank, and opposed 7 a.m. or 10 p.m. classes, making scheduling more difficult.

The deans also had to take the brunt of parental complaint when a student couldn't graduate on time, because a required class was not being offered.

Dr. Reis and I shared the same office for four years, but we never got on a first name basis. He was always Dr. Reis or Professor. I always felt comfortable in his presence, and felt that he was my friend and proctor. He taught the M-W-F classes and I liked the Tuesday-Thursday classes. That meant that I only had to be on campus two days a week. I had heard that Dr. Reis was very athletic. He played a mean game of tennis and was on the faculty basketball team. However, at the beginning of my fifth year on campus, I was shocked to learn that Dr. Reis had died of a massive heart attack on the tennis court Friday afternoon.

I dreaded going into the office the following Tuesday morning. I was sad, anticipating seeing all his notes and books, knowing that he would never use them again. However, when I opened the door, I was shocked again. Every trace of his existence was gone! Not a book and not a lecture note. Even the name on the door was gone.

The School of Business scheduled a memorial service on Thursday. As I waited quietly in the rush of the Forty-Niner Center, I recalled the many notes I would find on my desk with a word of encouragement or a favorable comment he had heard about my work.

As I sat there reminiscing, Margie, the Dean's assistant, sat down next to me and said, "You lost a good friend and protector." Then she related that she had sat in on the meeting of senior professors who had considered my appointment. She said there was a lot of concern because I would be a woman on a male staff, teaching all male students in a man's field of finance. "One professor even brought up your appearance. He described you as a small woman with a good figure, attractive, with dark hair, black snapping eyes and a feisty personality. He estimated that you were five or ten years younger than you are. And he seriously doubted if you could control your class."

"Dr. Reis reviewed your outstanding academic record and read glowing letters of recommendation from Illinois and Millikin Universities. He iterated the many achievements, like winner of Illinois Better Speakers contest as a young girl, voted Best Teacher in Illinois, winner of the Ford Foundation Award and others."

Margie took my hand and continued. "You know Dr. Dunyon, who taught investment classes. He said the department depended upon the good will and support of several stock brokerages in the community. He doubted they would look favorably on the appointment of a woman to teach students that they might want to hire." I told Margie that some of the brokers were my best supporters and even sent their new hires to my seminars. The administration is well aware of that now," she replied. "The very strong support of Dr. Reis swung the vote your way."

Reminiscing

Over the years, I was aware of a slightly negative bias on the part of Dr. Dunyon as I proposed new projects, started new student activity, or took my students on sponsored field trips to the NY Stock Exchange. Years after I had retired, I was honored by a new Dean. The Forty-Niner Newspaper had followed my career after retirement as I traveled the world working for the United Nations and serving as the spokeswoman for the American Bankers Association. On that day I was allowed to carry the mace as I led the graduates to their seats. Then I stood on the platform and distributed the diplomas to the graduates as they walked across the stage to get their diplomas amid the many flash bulbs of proud parents and friends of the graduates.

I stood beside the Dean and the trustees to congratulate the grads.

Originally, I had been asked to place hoods over their heads and drape them around the graduate's shoulders. My short stature soon made it obvious that the grads had to almost get on their knees before I could "hood" them. Quickly the Dean, who was 6-feet 3-inches tall, took my place. The grads and the audience had a good laugh. Later that evening at a black tie dinner, I was introduced as "the woman who broke the glass ceiling for women in business." It was appropriate, since the student who took top academic honors was a woman in the finance department. How wonderful! I thought silently,

You go girl!

CHAPTER 17

In this chapter, Nana remembers the O'Brien family, who lived in house #4 in their cul-de-sac in Buena Park. They were as Irish as their name implies, but I will let her tell you the story.

Scared to Death: A Lesson Too Well Learned

Shawn O'Brien's parents left Belfast when he was three-years-old and migrated to the United States to settle near Beloit. When I first knew him, he was probably in his late forties. Shawn was a picture perfect Irishman—handsome, broad shouldered, and brawny. A stevedore by profession with a glorious tenor voice. He sang as he worked, much to the delight of the other "wharf rats" as his fellow dock workers were called. He was much in demand whenever an Irish singer was needed.

One Saturday night, all the neighbors carpooled to Tustin, where Shawn was preforming at the opening of The True Irish Pub. His performance made all of us proud to call him friend and neighbor. His wife, Bridget, was a third generation Irish American. She was a typical pretty Irish lass with strawberry blond hair and piercing blue eyes. She made a striking contrast to Shawn with his dark black curly hair and piercing dark brown eyes. They had dated some during high school, but weren't what today's kids call "an item."

After graduation from high school, Shawn joined the Marines and served in the Pacific. Bridgette went to a local trade school and became a stenographer. She found employment with the Beloit Social Services, and eventually worked on cases of abused and missing children. They met again at a mixer for returning vets and began dating.

After a few months they decided to wed and a typical boisterous wedding was held. Shawn sang an Irish love melody at the altar to his blushing bride. He, like so many other servicemen who had traveled through California on their way to the Pacific War Zone, wanted to make California their home. Shawn and Bridget pooled their resources and with help from both sets of extended families set out for California. They settled in Orange County and soon found employment.

After many years of trying, and almost giving up, they had a son and called him Brian O'Brien. He was a beautiful child with curly, strawberry red hair and green eyes, perhaps a throwback to some past generation. He had perfect facial features and almost perfect alabaster skin. Bridget quit work and devoted her time to caring for the child for whom they had waited so long.

One day during the Christmas season, Bridget, our kids, and I decided to go shopping. I was still having trouble getting into the Christmas spirit in this very warm, dry, desert air. Why was that? We all know that the birth of Christ was in such an arid, desert climate, but I still missed the snow. Not for long. When we opened the doors of the mall, we were greeted with a winter wonderland. Cotton snow was everywhere—snow covered pine trees, automated deer, and other forest creatures all combined to bring back precious memories.

We headed for another section of the mall that featured Santa Clause and his sleigh flying through the air. This family, who had never experienced a white Christmas, liked Santa Clause the best. Bridget had dressed Brian in a lightweight green suit, which brought out the green of his eyes, and a very faint tone of pink in his skin. He received a lot of attention and smiles as he walked throughout Santa Land with Bridget right behind him.

Eventually we headed for the shopping areas. At one time, Bridget released Brian's hand while she returned a garment to the rack. He walked a few steps away and stopped in the aisle. An attractive, white haired lady in a colorful summer dress and pumps strolled by and lightly patted Brian's head.

He started screaming, "She touched me! She touched me!" Bridget tried to comfort him. The mall guard had restrained the elderly woman, who was trying to explain that it was just an innocent, admiring reaction to an attractive child. Had I not been there to back up her explanation, she might have been in serious trouble. The doctor had to be called for the frightened older lady and the three-year-old Brian who was in a panic shock.

On the way home, Bridget explained to me that she had worked on many horrible cases of child abuse and was deathly afraid for her son. She had cautioned him over and over again to scream if anyone touched him. She had unintentionally transferred her fear of people to the child. In the days and weeks that followed, I noticed that Brian was never alone or allowed to play with others. I cautioned my husband, who was very affectionate, not to touch Brian. Brian seemed too perfect (fragile even) for this rough and tumble world.

During the following May, the O'Brien family joined other members of his union on a weekend trip to the nearest national forest. This treasured and prized park had been enhanced by the government and local clubs with the addition of hiking trails, caves, and small streams. Bridget said she did not want to go for fear that something bad would happen to Brian in such a "wild" place, but Shawn wanted to be a part of the gang. Did she have a premonition?

Reluctantly, she packed a first aid kit with lotions to protect Brian's sensitive skin from bites and scratches.

Missing

Saturday morning, Bridget was helping the other women clean up after breakfast. Brian was sitting on the bench beside the table. Suddenly Bridget began screaming that Brian was missing. A quick search of the immediate vicinity yielded no trace of him. After the first few minutes, Bridget kept saying that she had never taken her eyes off him. But she must have. He was gone. Could some other child have led him away? Did he follow some other children? How far could a four-year-old get in a few minutes? Or did some adult snatch him away? Some of the other women swore that they had seen him at the table minutes before Bridget had missed him. A full scale search began and continued all day and that night.

By Sunday, the Search and Rescue teams had been called to organize an inch-by-inch search. Bridget had gone into a catatonic shock and was brought home. The media were on the story. Offers of help came in from all sections of Orange County. We neighbor women took turns sitting with Bridget, although we couldn't do much good. She would neither speak nor eat.

Jim and the other men spent day and night in organized searches.

The team captains concluded that Brian was not in the park. The police were now treating it as a criminal abduction. Shawn did not want the search stopped because he believed Brian would have screamed if touched by a stranger.

A reporter interviewed me because he had heard about the mall panic attack and I had been listed as a witness. I agreed that Brian would have screamed if touched unless somehow the attacker had been able to stifle his screams.

On the fourth day, the search dogs and their trainers had been flown in. Within hours, a small terrier entered a man-made cave and came out barking furiously. The trainer shouted that the dog had found something. Eager hands tore at the cement and rocks that had been used to create the little cavelike structure until it was big enough for an adult to enter. The desperate efforts by the men to reach Brian were too late. They found him—dead! What happened may never be known.

For days afterward the questions chased each other around and around. Why? When? How? The coroner's report only left these questions unanswered as they ruled the death "accidental" based on the known facts. The crime scene had been so destroyed by the efforts of the rescuers that there was no way to tell what really happened.

After the funeral, the TV trucks left as did members of the family from Beloit. The very large number of flowers that filled our cul-de-sac were taken away and life returned to normal. But not normal as it had been.

Shawn returned to work, but was never heard to sing again. Bridget wandered in that empty house and refused all attempts to include her in any activity. The sight of their dark, brooding house made me long for the time just a few weeks ago when we could have expected Shawn to burst out of the front door with Brian on his shoulders and break into a loud, happy song for the sheer joy of living. Normally on a bright day in May, neighbors would have been exchanging greetings, laughing, and planning barbecues and pool parties.

Somehow, it seemed disrespectful for us to laugh or carry on. Even the dogs seemed silent.

The friendly little blue collar neighborhood in Buena Park never did seem to recover from the O'Brien tragedy, and a somber mood spread through the homes. That atmosphere, paired with the need to be closer to the university, started my family's search for a new home in a more affluent neighborhood.

CHAPTER 18

My grandparents had always stated that they had been the original "yuppies." They were always moving onward and upward, conquering new challenges and terrain, and always "trading up."

Nana never could swallow the word "no" very well and this trait paired with her huge dreams, unconventional ideas, and pure tenacity propelled her from her $20,000.00 home in Buena Park into a million dollar home in Huntington Harbor.

Moving on Up

We were very comfortable in our home in Buena Park, but more and more I needed to be closer to the campus. I had been promoted to the graduate faculty. Most of the students were engineers or others who were working on an MBA degree. Because these students worked full time, classes were held from 7 p.m. to 10 p.m. and I had to travel the forty-five mile round trip at midnight— ouch! Also, Jim had just accepted a lecture appointment at a private college in Irvine, twenty-five miles south of USC. Patricia, now eighteen, would be attending USC; children of faculty members get free tuition and other perks. It was time to move.

In the summer of 1967, I started traveling the major roads radiating from USC. Huntington Harbour, about six miles south, fascinated me. It was an engineering marvel. Emulating the Dutch, the developer had created land out of water, thus proving the statement false, "God created only so much land, and when it is gone, there will be no more."

Military bases, public parks, and protected wet lands, made oceanfront land for home development practically non-existent.

This "slough" as the British call it, lay dormant for many years. It flooded at high tide and became a muddy morass at low tide. A marine engineer and a major developer from Los Angeles secured funding, permits, and clearance from innumerable governmental agencies to develop the land.

This, they explained, was the most difficult and time consuming part of the project; creating the project would be easy. Their plan was to build eight huge islands, "fingers" and interconnecting roads. Each finger was a huge concrete bulwark reaching down to bedrock and hollow in the middle. The surrounding land was then dredged and the salty earth was used to fill the finger. Thus they created boat traffic lanes connecting the eight fingers upon which the waterfront homes were built.

Each finger had five home sites (100 by 100 feet), a total of forty homes. Six years later the first homes were ready for occupancy.

By 1967 most of the homes were sold, but they were holding open houses by appointment and I signed up for one. The model home was #5 Admiralty. The first thing that caught my attention was the trees growing out of the top of the one story home. The road side of the home sported a huge, elaborately carved double door located in the center of the exterior wall, which appeared to be a solid stone wall painted to look like marble with a faint pink tint.

The open door revealed a glass wall surrounding an interior courtyard. There were palm trees of differing heights, bushes and pots of red geraniums. A landscaper, with a sense of humor, had put a pine tree front and center. My immediate thought was that it would make a wonderful Christmas tree.

The foyer was devoid of decoration, excepting for an unusual ceiling hugging crystal chandelier. The large, two-foot tile squares looked like Italian marble. The first room on the right was something I had always wanted in a home—a real library. Since the room had no exterior windows, there were book shelves on three sides with the fourth side wide open to the courtyard. A small, Louis XIV desk and matching chair, upholstered in a patterned material in various shades of red and pink, were the room's only furniture. The bookcases were strategically filled with leather bound volumes, with indirect lighting illuminating them. I sighed and thought, I would love to spend time here.

Next was a dining room with a massive table and twelve chairs.

Imagine! They appeared to be centuries old. The wood had faded to a soft gray, and it was nicked and scratched, adding authenticity to its age. However, the original upholstery was replaced with the red to pink patterned material.

This room, like the library, had three windowless walls housing built in hutches, breakfronts, and glass shelving holding sets of china, stemware, and elegant collectibles. Cabinets below the shelves held linen, silverware, serving trays, and covered dishes. The fourth wall was open to the glassed in courtyard. The only visible door opened to a half bath with a skylight. I had never seen skylights before, and immediately decided that I wanted skylights in my next home.

The next room was the kitchen with a window facing the water. It had gleaming white appliances and a small dining alcove. Following the marblelike tile path around the courtyard to the ocean side of the home, we came to the great room measuring about fifty feet long. A great room was also a new concept to me, replacing a living room and a family room. The water side of this room held solid sliding glass doors, while the opposite side faced the courtyard. That left only two small walls for pictures or background for furniture. I'm sure the interior decorator viewed this room as a nightmare or at least a challenge.

The interior decorator had decided to put deep pile gray carpet with pink undertones over about half the floor. This person chose a small, white baby grand piano as a focal point. Throughout the rest of the room, the decorator chose French style chaise lounges and placed small conversation centers with three or four chairs and a high table.

When stepping through the sliding glass doors, it was easy to realize why people loved living close to water. The deck ran the length of the house and was decorated with colorful beach chairs in shades of red. Clay pots with red geraniums warned visitors away from the edge of the deck. It was low tide when I was there so the gang plank slanted downward to the dock. Each site had two large, round cement piles (posts) to which the dock was cleverly attached. A heavy metal U-shape bar was fastened to the dock and loosely circled the pile. This allowed the dock and boat to rise and fall with the tide.

Although the nearest neighbor was over a mile away, the boaters going under Pacific Coast Highway on their way to the ocean, passed right by the house.

The master bedroom offered a breath-taking view of the water, with the bed on an elevated platform. Like the other rooms, it was open to the courtyard. Where's the privacy, the bath, the toilet? I wondered. Again the developer was very ingenious. Ten feet from the outer wall he had built a second wall with concealed openings. Touch the right spot and the doors slide open to reveal a bath, a toilet and a huge dressing room. Each of the bedrooms had a similar set up. Wow! The guest bedroom had a queen bed and the last one had twin beds.

As I left that fabulous house with the million dollar price tag, I knew there was no way we could buy such a home, unless we won the lottery.

But wait! Maybe . . . I've had an idea.

CHAPTER 19

This house was before my time; however, Nana called this her outside/in house. When I asked her what she meant by that she explained that traditional homes were surrounded outside by trees, shrubs, bushes, vines, grassy lawns, and flower beds, but in this house the trees, shrubs, bushes and vines were inside, as the house was built right up to the lot-line.

As aesthetically impressive as this house was, Nana said it was built for looks, but it wasn't so great to live in. As you read the next chapter, you'll understand why my grandfather said, "I mortgaged my future, only to live in a closet!"

Moving on In

After my visit to Huntington Harbour, I fantasized about owning that unique home. Could we do it? Should we do it? I remembered Grandfather's warning, "Not a borrower be." After further debating I told myself, *Forget it.*

But that was easier said than done. A couple of weekends later, we all visited the house again. While Jim and Pat were exploring this unusual, professionally decorated house in awe and wonder, I talked to the selling agent. She said there were still four houses for sale in the development, and that the price had been reduced from $1 million to $950,000; the developers were anxious to sell. Best of all, I learned that the V.P. of marketing for Unique Homes, Inc. was in Los Angeles. Then God smiled on me. The realtor gave me Mr. William's number, something that was only given out if she had a hot prospect, and thus I could avoid the layers of secretaries. Also, she told me they were cutting her open houses to two a month, or every other Sunday afternoon. I was shocked to learn how expensive it was for the company to maintain the home for open-house days. The bill to keep the windows clean came to one week of my salary!

That night our family discussed the pros and cons of making an attempt to purchase the house. For Jim's real estate business, the more affluent southern Orange County address would be a plus. Patricia could live at home and avoid the long commute to CSU. Since the house was only six miles south along Pacific Coast Highway from CSU, both of our commute distances would be reduced from a seventy-nine mile round trip to less than twelve miles. As well, the water front property was very desirable—and scarce—along the Southern California coast, so we might experience some price appreciation.

On a Monday morning in early October, I called the number I had been given, and told his private secretary that I was a hot prospect. That got me connected to Mr. William. After introducing myself, I said something like this: "I want to buy your model home in Huntington Harbour. I can't afford it, but I have an idea that will benefit both of us. I will be in L.A. Wednesday and I can meet you at 2:30. Is that convenient?" As he was trying to process my rapid fire statements, he mumbled something that I took for consent. I immediately said, "Thank you, I'll see you Wednesday" and hung up. The next call was to his secretary and she booked that appointment on his calendar. In the interval, I learned everything I could about Unique Homes, Inc., contacted a bank, and the lender confirmed a commitment for a $450,000 loan.

Creative Selling

At our meeting on Wednesday, I pointed out to Mr. William that the model home was a *used* home. By their advertisements, 2500 people had toured it since its grand opening. The home was a dead weight and wasn't a money-making property on their books. I would buy the home, giving them some badly needed cash, and offered to let the company continue to use it as a model. With a twenty-four hour notice, we would make the home available for showing, furnished model, at any time during the next two years.

I pointed out they had a buyer now, and in two more years the economy would be entering a downturn, so they would have trouble selling a used house. After about three hours, we had worked out a deal. We would pay $650,000 with $450,000 borrowed and $200,000 of our money. My family would pay utilities, but the company would pay for window washing. We would leave every other Sunday, so they could prepare for the open house. It was a win-win situation for both of us.

Over the next weeks both sides worked rapidly to iron out many details of a shared house. We also had to sell our home. That proved easy to do since it was priced at the median of $125,000. We were also buying the new house furnished, so we sold our old house furnished. After three weeks of signing loan papers and legal documents with Unique Homes, Inc., we were ready to move on in.

Necessary Adjustments

When we walked into our new home the first day, we simply couldn't believe it was ours. Over the next week or so, we were thrilled to find nuances that were simply not available in a "normal" house. But after a few weeks realty set in. The house was built for looks but wasn't very comfortable to live in. I spent a lot of my time at home in the study. The elegant French desk with its inkwell and quill pen was not very practical, but when I swiveled the chair around to face what seemed like a solid wall and touched a button. The doors opened to reveal an eight-by-five foot desk with five drawer filing cabinets on either side. There were several desk top height electrical and phone outlets, an innovation that I wondered why more builders didn't use. Why put the outlets eight inches off the floor and cut off easy reach of the computers, copiers, and fax machines?

I found many of the books were false imitations of leather bound volumes of classic works. We added our own thirty volumes of the Great Books and the twenty-four volumes of the Encyclopedia Britannic.

The massive dining room table with its twelve chairs was used only on formal occasions. Our family preferred the kitchen, and there was just enough room for our dinette set. Our kitchen was the most useful and most used room in the house. It seemed cozier because it was more enclosed. The kitchen window offered a great view of the water, and we could often see water fowl swimming by. The living room was not designed for living in with its wall-to-wall glass doors opening up to the deck, and the other wall of glass surrounding the courtyard. Also, there wasn't a comfortable chair in the room.

However, I loved the white baby grand, which was a player piano that became a regular one with a touch of a switch. With its electronic discs, we could enjoy symphony music at any time. Jim could play almost anything by ear and enjoyed playing.

The fact that all the rooms opened onto the inner courtyard offered a level of comfort. However, with the master bedroom having one wall of glass doors opening onto the deck and waterfront, we lost all sense of privacy. The bed was elevated on a one-foot platform, offering us an exquisite view. It was the only room in the house that had curtains that were made of shimmering mesh material. They allowed us to bask in the moonlight on the water.

However, if the lights were on, the boaters could see into the bedroom.

Within weeks we had vacated the master for the guest room. Jim soon brought in a comfortable recliner, a TV, a lamp, a small bookcase, and desk. It was home sweet home. But it really cluttered up the room and ruined the decor. Because of our agreement to let the house be shown any time with a twenty-four hour notice, his hide away had to be hidden. After a few months of this, we cleared out the dressing room, and made a permanent den for him.

Jim grumbled that he had mortgaged his future only to live in a closet.

Pat, who had the third bedroom, was a light sleeper and wanted no lights in her room. On the first night she discovered that the glass wall to the inner courtyard flooded the room with moonlight. On her way home from school, she stopped at a local drugstore and bought a number of different sleeping masks. In spite of these adjustments we had to make, we were proud of our new home and began to entertain.

CHAPTER 20

It was around this time that my parents met under unusual and comical circumstances. My father (a business major) was enrolled in and unsuccessfully struggling through my Nana's econ class at CSU. My father (also an unconventional problem solver) found out that Dr. Belt had a very attractive daughter, who happened to grade the class papers for her mother. Soon my father had tracked her down and procured a date.

Bill was big man on campus, and part of the fraternity. He had a charismatic personality, and piercing blue eyes that gleamed with the spark of excitement and mischief that his devilish shaped brows seemed to confirm. My mother, Patricia, was shy and reserved, but anxious for friends and fun, she was thrilled to be going out with Bill to the Frat party.

Mom had a fabulous time (as she recounts) until my father's eloquent proposal that she make sure he passed her mother's econ class. In return she would be invited, included, and escorted to all of the coveted social functions. My mother was appalled! She dumped her drink over the top of his swollen head and stormed out. This incident started the beginning of a volley of petty assaults between them that spanned well over a year before the two's fiery attacks softened and they succumbed to the underlying passion that had existed between them.

Mom and Dad quickly began a whirlwind romance. About eight months after they had been dating, my father asked my grandparents if he could take my mother to Colorado on a ski trip. However, my grandparents stated that it was unacceptable for an unmarried woman to go off overnight with a man, and the idea was immediately vetoed. Several weeks later my father proposed to my mother. They announced their engagement and were married and honeymooned in Colorado as planned. This led to the next phase of my grandparent's lives—becoming empty-nesters.

Emptying the Nest

When the chairman of the finance department visited one evening, he made a casual remark about our house being an ideal place for the department's Christmas party. We began to plan and enlarged the party to include the complete School of Business. I contacted the Dames, the wives of senior professors, who planned the social activities for the school. After a couple of them came for tea, they were very excited. The party was normally held in the Commons, which was difficult to decorate in a Christmas theme.

The ladies agreed to furnish food and decorations, if I would provide my lovely home. I was happy to do so.

I then learned that Unique Homes Inc. decorated a home each year, and had a huge party for the media, the politicians, and the movers and shakers of Orange County. Of course, it was held at my house. The professional decorators came the first week of December and created a true winter wonderland, with white lights and large reflective white crystal balls and bells.

It was breath-taking in its simplicity. This made me realize that "less is best."

They even brought a tastefully decorated cruiser to our dock, and their piano player was incredible! We invited the pianist back to play at our party; how I wish I could play half as well as he did.

When the Dames saw the elaborate decorations, they decided to spend more on food and entertainment. They also hired a good combo from the music department for a short sing-along. I believe that getting to know other members of the school helped me when I came before the RTP (retention, tenure, and promotion) board. In the meantime, we threw our own party for friends of neighbors and clients, or hope-to-be clients. Pat also invited some of her friends, but I think they were too awe-struck to relax and have a good time.

We were invited to the black-tie party given by Unique Homes during the Christmas break, and we and the house received a lot of publicity. And so ended our first Christmas in our new home.

Raising Funds

Early in the New Year I joined a fund rising committee for the O.C. Philharmonic Society. The lighted cruiser that Unique Homes had docked at our home gave me an idea. At our summer fund raising meeting, I proposed a Christmas Boat Parade with prizes for the best decorated boats and houses. We could charge fees for boat rides to see the decorated houses, and later sell a box meal and hot cider at the Club. Thus we could raise money for the Society.

At first, it was very simple with owner decorated boats. Later, as the Harbour expanded and more affluent people moved in, most boats and homes were professionally decorated. It became big business. For years, I served on a three-person judging group to award the prizes. Even after we had moved out of the Harbour, I came back to judge during the Christmas Boat Parade.

Home Away from Home

CSU was located in Long Beach, one of the West Coast's biggest ports, and had become noted for its international student studies. I had many such students in my classes. I realized that most of them were lonely during our holidays, especially Christmas and New Year's. We decided to invite some of them for a typical Christmas dinner.

As time passed and I began to have more and more foreign students in my classes, I decided to host a party for each class in my home one time per semester. Often American type food presented the foreign students with challenges. I recall two occasions. Once I served corn-on-the-cob and a student from India asked, "Isn't this what you feed cows?" I had to explain that this was a specially grown tender corn for humans. Another time I served artichokes and noticed a student from Bora Bora chewing and chewing and chewing in bewilderment. I showed him how to drag the leaf between his teeth to extract the pulp and then discard the leaf in the container beside his plate.

Soon, they were laughing and filing their containers with the discarded leaves of this strange vegetable.

One Sunday, Lek Limtanacool, a student from a large family in Thailand where I had visited, felt that he knew me well enough to make a suggestion. He had brought a large covered bowl of balls of sticky rice. After watching the Oriental students eat those hard unseasoned balls of rice, I said goodbye to Uncle Ben's rice as I realized what my guests wanted was a taste of home.

Wedding Bliss

The highlight of the 1967 Christmas season was the marriage of our daughter, Patricia, to William G. McGill of Massachusetts. The actual ceremony was held at the Wayfarer's Chapel on the L.A. Peninsula, designed by Frank Lloyd Wright. It was a very popular site for those wanting a memorable wedding.

On this pre-Christmas Sunday, there were five weddings scheduled.

Ours was at 5 p.m. and we had seventy-five minutes to assemble the wedding party, wedding guests, perform the ceremony, take the photos, and leave before the next wedding party arrived. Pat's bridesmaids, including her cousin from Illinois and Bill's sister from Massachusetts, were dressed in shimmering red gowns and carried a bouquet of white roses. Pat's gown was a beautiful white satin and veil. She carried a spray of red roses. Jim, Bill, and his best men and groomsmen were in black tuxes with a red cummerbund. I wore a patterned eggshell crème long dress. All in all, we made some attractive pictures.

Meanwhile back at the house, invitees for the reception were being hosted by recruited friends and neighbors. After a forty-five minute ride, the wedding party and guests arrived to hosts of well-wishers and the party was in full swing. The caterers were busy and the bartender was extra busy. Two of my neighbors in festive holiday gowns were manning punch bowls at each end of the massive dining table, and the twelve chairs were in use. Everything was under control, so the bride and groom and all relatives formed an informal line to say goodbye to those leaving and hello to those arriving.

Because of the parking shortage, we had staggered the arrival times for the reception guests. All too soon the time came for the bride and groom to make preparations to leave. Pat and all the younger guests went out to the deck where Pat threw her bridal bouquet. Her unmarried cousin caught it by prearrangement, I believe. Pat and William were then ready to leave.

My mother, from a conservative Baptist background, got my attention and said in a distressed voice, "Virginia, she's in her room changing clothes and he is in there with her." I said that they had been married for several hours.

She reluctantly nodded, but added, "It still doesn't seem decent."

Pat and Bill emerged in matching ski suits; they were planning to spend their honeymoon on the ski slopes. We all followed them out on the deck and wished them well as they descended the gang plank to a waiting boat that would take them about a mile up the coast to the Baron Hotel, where they would spend the night. We had also arranged rooms there for our out-of-town guests. I later learned that most of our younger guests had gone to the Baron Hotel as well. I wonder how much sleep, if any, Pat and Bill got before they left for a week of skiing.

Changes in Life

With an empty nest and the excitement of planning a wedding over, we soon returned to the business of making our fortune in this land-of-milk-and-honey. Jim obtained his real estate license and also a California insurance certificate. Now when he sold a house, he could insure it as well. I also passed the stock broker license and hung my license with a former student, who had created his own brokerage. I would now be privy to breaking news and could trade stocks in my account, and I also received a lot of information and supplies that I could share with my classes.

When our two-year agreement with Unique Homes was up, we gradually began to turn this awe inspiring house into a more comfortable home. The demand for and the scarcity of waterfront land had made our home very valuable. The massive migration to California had not abated, and there was a huge demand for affordable houses. Developers were buying up orange groves, turning struggling farmers into overnight millionaires. Several of these farmers became my clients as they toiled with their new wealth. Jim was surprised to hear several of them express regret because they sold out, preferring the simple, hard working life they had always known.

I began working for O.C. Development Agency as they tried to monitor this rapid eastern movement. Infrastructure and especially freeways had to be planned and built. The building permit department's personnel had tripled and then quadrupled. Those of us on the Development Committee were full-time employees elsewhere, and we advised the OCDC on a part-time basis. But the demand for our time was getting so great that I considered resigning.

The university system was considering creating a new university on the huge Irvine Ranch to serve the many new communities that were being carved out of the inland ranches and orange groves. Jim was beginning to believe that his real estate business should be relocated further east where the biggest developments were occurring. Should we begin looking eastward for a home site and cash in on the increased value of our Huntington Harbour home?

CHAPTER 21

I remember when Nana first moved into this house. I can remember being quite distraught that she was moving away from my Jessie.

Jessie was my first love. I was five-years-old and he was six. He proposed one Wednesday by way of cracker jack prize ring. I immediately accepted and we rode off together. I rode behind him on his big wheel; my dress flying high up around my ears and my pink ruffled panties waving in the wind.

Jessie had a big, big dog named Butch. He was of the Heinz 57 variety. I liked to ride him like a pony. Nana owned a teeny tiny Pekingese pup that was so funny and friendly that I named him Happy. We four gave the neighborhood much to laugh about. Those were fun days, but I'll let Nana tell you about them.

Moving on Out

During my tenth year at CSU and our seventh year at Huntington Harbour, we began to seriously consider joining the eastward migration inland and away from the coast. Status had changed for me, and it was no longer important that we live near the university. I was granted tenure (lifetime employment) during my third year, and was promoted to a full professorship during my fifth year. As a Full, I was expected to teach only three, three-hour classes and one hour of consultation per week—ten hours total. Also, as a full professor, I could select the hours I wanted to teach. Since I had been appointed to the graduate school, I taught mostly men who worked during the day and studied for their

MBA during the evenings. Thus I scheduled my classes for early evening or nights on Tuesday and Thursday.

During the other hours, the Full was expected to do research and publish. One professor counted his worth to the university by the number of lines published under his name in scholastic journals. However, only a few erudite individuals would read these journals, and fewer would understand what was written. But the old adage, "Publish or Perish," was still important in eastern universities. The western universities had adopted a more practical approach, and encouraged advisory service to the numerous developmental projects in a rapidly growing area.

My work with the O.C. Development Agency brought a lot of favorable publicity to the school. As communities and cities were developed inland, many social clubs and organizations sprang up and needed speakers for their meetings. I was in the Speakers' Bureau and was told that, after the school president, I was the most requested speaker. Thus, more and more of my time was spent inland rather than on the coast.

New Digs

Jim's real estate and insurance business was also moving east with the development. After a few weeks of on and off discussion, we decided to move on out and began going to open houses and studying the "homes for sale" ads.

Then God smiled on Jim.

A large developer had created a big PUD, Public Urban Development, on the border of Santa Ana, the capital of Orange County and Tustin. In order to promote sales of his homes, he had built a model home and a clubhouse. His original intention was to have the home buyers own and operate the clubhouse with its Olympic size pool accessible to all owners. However, when the developers took a survey of the buyers they found that the other owners did not want to use or pay for the clubhouse & pool. So he enclosed the model home and the clubhouse in a large fence and offered both for sale as a package.

Jim's real estate agency, along with others, was offered an above average commission for selling this unusual piece of property.

We decided that we could use the clubhouse in our business and gain a good tax write off. Now it was my job to finance it. Although our agreement with Unique Homes, Inc. had expired, they frequently arranged to show our home to visiting VIPs. I called and asked if they could sell our home. Within days, they were back with a buyer. When all the paperwork was finished for both houses, we had twice as much land and building for the price of our waterfront property!

Our home on Silver Maple Road lived up to our hopes. It was spacious and comfortable, not awe inspiring as the Huntington Harbour house had been, but more conventional and cheaper to maintain. The solar heated pool combined with the milder inland climate made the pool house a favorite for our grandchildren and our guests.

Soon after we moved in, my recently widowed sister came to live with us. She was a good housekeeper and a super cook. She made it so much easier for me and assuaged the guilt I was feeling over my neglect of my home and husband. She soon joined several groups such as the Single Adults at Crystal Cathedral and PWP (Parents without Partners), and it wasn't long before they were having some big parties at our house. The club house was seldom empty for long.

New Horizons

At the beginning of each school year, I would study the list of available grants or other opportunities for further study. I was looking for any grant that I might have a chance to win. One such grant was offered by the United Nations and dealt with the "Economics of Alternative Energy." I studied everything I could find about alternative energy and the United Nations. I applied, crossed my fingers, and won a six-week expense paid project to study the feasibility of further research on the development of the volcanic islands of the southern Pacific Ocean, including New Zealand. This meant traveling for me, something I was looking forward to, knowing that my household was in the capable hands of my sister.

An aside to this story, I want to relate a question that I was asked by an elderly lady at a "conversations with the author." She asked, "Were you ever panicked or afraid as you went from island to island? I would be." Yes, I remembered one frightening experience:

I was assigned to a small island about 400 miles west of the big island of Tahiti. After landing at Tahiti, I boarded a two-passenger jumper plane. Either the pilot had taken a vow of silence or he didn't speak English. We communicated by sign language. He signed for me to board and be seated. As the silent pilot and I traveled over miles and miles of ocean, I began to be very uneasy. Eventually we saw a small dot in the ocean and he descended to land on the dirt runway. He left the plane idling and practically pushed me out and just left me standing as he roared down the runway and up into the sky. I watched the plane get smaller and smaller and I panicked. The airport terminal on this small island was a flat roof with four supporting corners. The only seat in the terminal was a bale of hay. I couldn't see any sign of habitation and I wondered if I had been abandoned in the middle of nowhere. After what seemed to be forever, but was in reality more like a half hour, I heard and saw a modified jeep approaching. I breathed a silent prayer of thanks.

The driver of the jeep was Zongi, a relative of the local governor. He was to be my interpreter. Zongi had been taught English by the Mormon missionaries.

While we waited, he had hundreds of questions, or so it seemed. Why was I, a woman, traveling alone? Did I have a husband and children? Were there many women like me in America? How strange. Where did I live? What did my house look like?

When I described the two houses and the pool he shook his head in amazement. After my questions to the Governor and other officials were answered, we went back to wait for the small jumper plane I had come in on and he continued the barrage of questions. As I was leaving I said, "If you are ever in America come and visit us." Months later, I was called out of class to take a call from Jim. He had received a call from a very, very black man called Zongi. Jim had been ordered to send a driver to the Los Angeles airport to pick him up, and said that I had invited him to stay with us.

"He's here. What do you want me to do with him?" Jim asked.

Needless to say we had a strange week. Zongi seemed surprised that American streets weren't paved in gold, and that we didn't have as many servants in a house that was bigger than the palace in his country. Although he was darker than anyone I had ever seen, he was very prejudiced against Afro-American blacks. He said that when American ships came into their port, the captains were not allowed to let our blacks come ashore. Talk about reverse discrimination! He seemed disappointed that we could not take him to see the wonderful things he had read about such as the Grand Canyon, San Francisco, and even Canada. We did not live up to his expectations, and I resolved to be more careful when I issued an invitation in the future. But I never did learn, and we ended up with many foreign visitors and many interesting experiences.

We lived on Silver Maple Road until we retired. By then we were ready for something smaller.

CHAPTER 22

Nana was surprised at the various reactions of people when she told the story of going up in the freight elevator. Some were angry, but most considered it funny, and all considered it interesting. As you read this chapter you can judge for yourself.

Going Up in the Freight Elevator

Teaching is by far my favorite professional activity, but after that at a distant second, I enjoy grantsmanship. Usually after two or three weeks my classes have begun to gel and I start to haunt the libraries, searching for announcements of grants, projects, or research opportunities that I might qualify for and stand a chance to win. These grants are offered, with stipends, by governments, corporations, and professional groups, with the aim of having someone do the research and prepare a report, which they then use to secure funding.

Before I could hunt for a grant though, I had to develop smooth running classes. After a preliminary assessment of the scholarly attributes of the enrollees, I adjusted, if necessary, the vita, lesson plans, and presented it to the students. During the first two-week period, a student could drop a class without a penalty, and some did. I had a reputation for being a demanding teacher and a hard grader. But I was also very much a favorite teacher. In fact, one of my prized ego possessions is a dog-eared copy of "The Forty-Niner" the student newspaper, which named me as one of the top ten professors out of 2200 in the entire system. Accompanying my name was this statement, "Knows more about more things than anyone, but if you want an 'A', run like hell." That was in the late '70s, and a student revolt was sweeping across college campuses.

Although CSU did not experience the violent revolts and sit-ins of some more radical colleges, we did have an active group, calling itself "Students for Democratic Activity." Most schools had faculty dominated RTP committees, which determined retention, tenure, and promotion for all teachers. The SDA demanded that 'right' for students. They conducted a massive survey of all former and current students of each professor and vowed to publish a list of the best and the worst, or those they wanted fired. Although some faculty members adopted a devil-may-care attitude, most of us were concerned about our grading by our students. Needless to say, I was surprised and very delighted to be named among the ten best, by student choice.

Another demand of the SDA was the right to go into any class to discuss student democracy issues that they considered more relevant than dull lectures in history, Latin, or economics. The administration had to bow to this demand and order campus police not to interfere. My classes were not invaded, either due to happenstance or to George Brown, a burly black police student. For some reason, George and his pals decided to protect my classes.

Unfortunately, George had more brawn than brain, and I had to close my eyes and give him a minimal passing grade.

A New Grant

During the summer and early fall, libraries gathered and collated offers of grants from various sources. In my free time, I traveled to most of the libraries in Southern California, searching through hundreds of grant announcements. Most of them were for science and engineering or liberal arts, but once in a while, I found one that excited me, like the one offered by the American Securities Institute, ASI, which invited professors and professionals to apply for a three week, all expenses paid trip to New York to attend the Forum on Finance. The purpose was to provide a forum for those in the profession to have a hands-on exchange of ideas. This forum was sponsored by exchanges like NYSE and ASE, by investment bankers, like *Goldman Sachs*, by over-the-counter firms, and many other firms in the security industry. The brochure said that thirty applicants would be invited to participate.

I learned everything I could about the members of the ASI, wrote and rewrote my letter of application, obtained several letters of recommendation, crossed my fingers, and sent it off with a silent prayer. Three months later, when I had almost given up hope, I received a letter from a John Wellman inviting me to attend the Forum on Finance. In the meantime, I continued to teach my classes, do research, write articles for financial journals, and write a weekly column for the Newport News. I even advised women from Newport Beach as they organized the Newport Women's Bank.

At a speech to the Women's Club the previous year, I had pointed out that all the banks in Newport were controlled by men, but that 67.5 percent of those deposits were owned by women, either through divorce or death of their spouse. These wealthy society women decided to create their own bank and become bankers. Returning to thoughts of my upcoming trip to the Finance Forum in New York, I sought the advice of some of the wealthiest of these society women to help me assemble a wardrobe that would be professional but suitable for muggy New York weather. In April, Mr. Wellman sent a packet of information outlining our schedule of visitations to the major financial institutions in New York City, starting on June 15th. My birthday was June 6th and I considered this a wonderful birthday gift.

New York Finance

June finally arrived and I was making plans with my family to be away for three weeks. As usual, they were very supportive, and Jim drove me to Los Angeles to catch the plane to New York on Friday the 13th. Mr. Wellman had planned for us to spend the weekend recuperating and getting to know each other.

When he met me at the airport, I sensed something strange when he asked me twice if I were the Dr. McKemie-Belt, who was attending the

Forum on Finance. I understood his uncertainty when I learned that I was rooming with a male professor from Omaha, Nebraska, who had been recommended by Warren Buffet. Ouch! Yet another problem encountered by a woman in a man's world of finance. He had not looked at any of the references and just assumed that all the invitees were men. That error was corrected, and we got to know each other over dinner and explored our environs.

My hotel was located near the old St. John cemetery and chapel, and on Sunday some of the ASI attendees walked through the cemetery, reading the inscriptions on the tombstones, some dating back to the 1600s. We came out on a strangely quiet and deserted Wall Street. What a contrast we would find on Monday morning when we visited the NYSE, which was first on our schedule. We spent two days at the NYSE, and even though I had been there once before, I learned so much more about the frenzied activity and mounds of paper required to support the traders on the floor.

Each evening when we returned to our hotel, Mr. Wellman would give us a packet of papers describing the host for the next day. Our homework for the night was to fully understand the packet so that we could be conversant with all the information contained therein. Some of us soon organized study groups in the conference room, where we could order drinks and snacks and learn off the synergism of each other.

The weekends were ours to see some of New York's major attractions, like the Statue of Liberty. Mr. Wellman also somehow found scarce tickets to two Broadway shows. Unfortunately, there was more that we wanted to see and do than there was time to do it.

The next twelve week days were hectic and information packed as we moved from one financial institution to another. We took with us our material we had studied the night before in preparation for our visits, and received an almost equal amount of new material at each institution. Each one wowed us with their belief of their importance to the smooth running of the country's entire economy.

For example, the men from the Pimco Bond Fund stressed that without their work there would be no new infrastructure, no bridges, no roads and no airports. That night one of the professors noted he was beginning to suspect the forum was a big PR project. We were being subjected to an overload of information. How could I begin to share with my students even a fraction of what I had learned? An idea began to germinate in my mind: maybe I could begin to pressure the administration to let me teach a class titled something like "What You Need to Know About the New York Financial Institutions."

The brochure describing the Forum on Finance stated as its purpose, "To provide a place, an opportunity or a forum for the equal exchange of ideas between Wall Street and Main Street." I always tried to find some statement in the literature or in their speech that would be subject to two equally correct, but different conclusions. My purpose was to stimulate a lively discussion. An equal but personal purpose was to elicit comments like, "That's an insightful observation," or "Thank you for calling our attention to that point," or "I'm glad you asked." I wanted to make a favorable impression on the Financial VIPs; it's possible that one of them would do something or say something to enhance my career.

For example, a VP of Chase Manhattan Bank in New York wrote to the Chairman of the local Chase Bank, William McCully, and said, "What this country needs are more professors like the very intelligent, enthusiastic, and charming Dr. Virginia Belt of CSU." Mr. McCully, who sat on the Board of Directors of the entire California university system, forwarded the letter to the president of my school, expressing the Board's pleasure for his astuteness in hiring such a noteworthy professor. President Stephen Horn, who probably didn't know me from Adam before, did now, and he forwarded the letter to me along with sincere congratulations.

Up the Freight Elevator

The last Friday of the third week of the forum was scheduled as a wrap-up day, and it also happened to coincide with the annual meeting of the ASI, the American Security Institute, which had been the main sponsor. It had been planned that one of the professors attending the forum would give the luncheon address, saying a few words of thanks, and perhaps relating some interesting experiences or impressions. At dinner

Wednesday night, Mr. Wellman asked whom we wanted to represent the group at the luncheon. After much discussion, I was chosen to speak for the Group. Why? Because I talked so much? Because I was the only woman? More than likely, it was because Mr. Wellman, who had finally gotten around to reading my biography, pointed out that I had won the Illinois Better Speakers contest, that I had been a very successful Dramatics Director, and that the Speaker's Bureau reported that I was a most requested speaker for social and professional clubs in Southern California. Mr. Wellman gave me an outline of a speech appropriate for a crowd of two hundred of New York's finest. It was dull and bland and I determined to enliven it with some spicier comments.

Mr. Wellman escorted us to a very posh exclusive private club just off Wall Street and I entered with all the men. I was feeling very elegant in my peach colored coat dress by COCO with the Gucci accessories, which the high society Newport socialites had selected, assuring me that I would be well dressed anywhere, including the Exchange Club. I was standing at the bar getting ready to order the pre-luncheon drink, when I felt two hands on my arms, and before I could protest I was hustled out the massive doors to the sidewalk.

One of the bouncers said, "Weren't you told that women are never, never allowed in the Exchange Club?"

"No," I replied, adding they had a serious problem because I was the scheduled speaker for the day. They excused themselves and went seeking directions from higher authorities. When they returned, they took me around the back of the building to a freight elevator and when it opened up we entered a massive dining room complete with crested china and stemware. The heavy silverware on the gleaming white linen was embossed with an elegant "E."

A gentleman dressed in tails came in and apologized and asked me not to leave the room. In the meantime Mr. Wellman was frantically trying to find his speaker. He and others had seen me come in, but no one had seen me leave. Those bouncers were very good at removing undesirables quickly and quietly. The crowd grew bigger by the minute, and soon was over crowding the bar lounge and demanding entrance to the dining room. The MC curtly ordered Wellman to start even if he didn't have a speaker. The first guests entered the room, laughing and talking, but soon fell silent when they saw a lone woman sitting at the head table. I explained what had happened, and when the luncheon started about ten minutes late, Mr. Chapman described my misadventure, and vowed to lead the charge to change the ancient rules.

After my shortened speech, the members of the forum gathered around me as if in support. It was interesting to hear the reaction of the ASI.

Some were angry and threatened to boycott the Exchange Club. Some saw the humor in the situation when I said I was changing the title of my speech to "Up the Freight Elevator." The speech was not memorable, but the results would be. One man said that I had single handedly started the breakup of the all-male social clubs in New York City.

Surprising Events

After three hectic weeks on Wall Street, it was wonderful to return home to the relative quiet of Orange County, California. I had not signed up for summer classes, so I had the whole summer to catch up on family and community happenings. Soon after I arrived home, I received a wire from Mr. Wellman. He explained that in the spring, after he had scheduled the final luncheon for forum members at the Exchange Club, he was unaware that one of the attendees would be a woman. I chuckled and later called him to report that my misadventure had provided me with another interesting incident in my career as a woman in a man's field of finance. In fact, that incident proved beneficial to me in many ways. As the saying goes, I was able "to turn my scars into stars" and capitalize on the up-in-the-freight-elevator event.

When I returned to my office at CSU, I learned that the Speakers Bureau had received several requests for me to be the guest speaker at various events. They had tentatively accepted an invitation on my behalf from the Elks Club in two weeks. At that event, I recounted my experiences as a woman among thirty men, and I talked about the misadventure of being bounced from the exclusive all-man's Exchange Club, only to be readmitted via the freight elevator. The favorable reaction to my speech exceeded my highest expectations and I knew I had a winner. After my speech, three Elk members asked me to speak at other functions, thus my reputation grew.

Requests for me to speak doubled at the Speakers Bureau, and I made an average of one speech per week during the rest of that summer. My husband was right when he said that "I was singing for my supper."

Occasionally a program director would give me a $25 or $50 check for gas, but mostly it was pro bono.

Eventually reporters began to ask me for interviews about my experiences in New York. My scrapbook has several of these articles, and the titles reflect the opinion of the women reporters: "Posh Men's World Penetrated" and "Wall Street Invaded by Woman Professor." The headline from the *Los Angeles Times* in big, bold print urged "Women Arise." The body of the article told women to take a lesson from Mrs. J. Radford Belt, better known to the business world as Dr. Virginia McKemie-Belt.

That article received a lot of attention, perhaps because my picture and story shared the front page of the *View* with a picture and story of Charlie Chaplin, now white haired and rather feeble, as he accepted the Academy Award in his wheelchair. Reuters, a national syndicate for financial news, reported on the Forum on Finance and mentioned me as a guest speaker, but not a word about the elevator incident. They did, however, say that I was surprised and pleased to learn that Dr. Robert Mayer, who was my former Professor at the University of Illinois, was also an attendee. The editor of the *Register* heard me speak at a Rotary breakfast, and he titled his article "Going Up in a Freight Elevator."

CHAPTER 23

The dress codes of the many islands of the Pacific that my Nana visited were very important, and also very different. Nana said that she had to carry many different outfits to meet the varied cultural requirements. She always tried to carry two long, crushable crepe dresses so that she wouldn't run the risk of being thought of as a promiscuous, ugly American.

Ugly American — Inadvertently

My contact with the American Bankers Association had set up a tentative itinerary for a trip to Hong Kong to represent the ABA at the Asiatic Currency Unit meeting. One of the suggested segments was a flight on the Garuda Airlines. Using the atlas and an encyclopedia (this was before Google and other search companies made information available at the click of a mouse) I did some research.

Garuda is the national airline of the islands of Indonesia. I learned that passengers using Garuda were required to arrange a twenty-four hour layover on one of the Islands making up the nation of Indonesia. A map showed some of the islands to be Java, Sumatra, Lombork, and Bali. Bali! I stopped right there. I had loved the movie, *South Pacific*, and the pastoral scenes of Bali along with the haunting song, *Bali-Hi*. Whether the movie had actually been shot on Bali or on some sound stage in Hollywood, I didn't know. I also learned that the feeder plane came to Bali on a five-day interval.

Jim and I tried to take a vacation each year to someplace unique and different. Maybe I could arrange my schedule to include five days on Bali and he could go with me (at his own expense, of course). With the cooperation of my contact at the ABA, we were able to adjust the schedule to include the extra vacation.

Misshapen Hands

Jim and I were booked into the International Hotel near the airport, just outside the capital city of Denpasar. It was a typical, hi-rise Western hotel, looking very much out-of-place in the South Sea island setting. It was very modern and comfortable, however, and sported the normal bars, restaurants, gyms, and even a beauty salon. Their motto was "A Home Away From Home."

Every evening, the program director from Chicago presented lectures on the history and culture of Bali. We learned that Indonesia had been created from the unification of thirty-three islands by the Dutch. Such a diverse group of persons and cultures made for countless conflicts. Over time many of the Asiatic Indians migrated to Bali, and at this time, the island was dominated by the Asiatic Indians with the principle religion of Hindu.

Each evening, we were entertained by beautiful Balinese dancers, draped in flowing, multiple-colored saris. The dancers were teenagers, probably in their late teens. As is typical of Polynesian dancers, hand movements are a very important part of the dance. The young girl's hands, though very gracious, were misshaped. They all turned out at the top knuckle. After the second night's program, I asked the director about their hands. She explained that their culture considered the shape of the hand as a mark of beauty, and girls with those hands danced in hotels, clubs, temples, processions, and more. Mothers of pretty baby girls began stretching the muscles and tendons of the upper knuckles to make them grow into that backward position. I wondered what happened to those girls when they were too old to dance at about twenty-five-years-old. (I was reminded of the fate of Japanese women whose feet were bound to create fashionable, small feet. NATURALLY, they could not walk well and have servants do a lot of the tasks reserved for the wife.

Road Building Primitive Style

On our trip into Denpasar I found part of the answer. The town contained single lane streets without much traffic, no big box stores, and no bars or red light districts that I observed. Jim and I watched a road-building crew in action, something I could use in my economic classes as an example of primitive use of land, labor, and capital. An old truck brought a load of rocks and stopped in front of a group of men. Women then came up to the men with a flat basket on their heads. The men loaded the rocks in the flat basket, and women walked down the road to a hole, tipped their head, and dumped the rocks into the hole. They walked leisurely back to the rock pile for another load. I noticed that many of the women had the backward turning knuckle.

They used their palms to hold the flat baskets.

Honor without Waste

That night we saw another example of island economy. There was a processional of women with the flat baskets on their heads, but this time they held fruit. Our English speaking guide explained this processional was to honor a family member who had died. He said the more baskets of fruit, the more prayers the priests would say for the souls of the departed. As the fruit began to pile up, my Scottish soul began to rebel at the waste of food. When I expressed my feelings, the guide suggested we come back in about an hour and he would show us something interesting. We did and saw a big crowd waiting behind the temple, among them many of the women who had brought the fruit. Soon the back doors opened and the priests began passing out the fruit to the waiting crowd. It was an example of island practicality: honor without waste. I could use this example in my economics class as well.

Short Shorts—A No No

Guests at our hotel could rent mid-sized scooters for transportation.

Jim and I rented one and left early one morning to drive up Mt. Agung. That volcanic mountain erupted in 1963 and killed thousands. We were almost a quarter of a mile from the hotel when an old truck came barreling down the road heading straight for us. We ended up in the ditch. After we determined that no real damage had been done to us or the scooter, we resumed our trip, but with some changes. Jim remembered the "wrong" side of the road is the "right" one in most countries, and when I got back on I spread my legs around his buttocks, and held on for dear life.

As we traveled further up the mountain, it seemed that we had left civilization behind. The higher we traveled the hotter the scooter got, and Jim had to stop to let it cool. It was then that we learned the forests beside the road were populated. People materialized around us and many offered a piece of fruit. At one pit stop a young boy said, "Hi, Pard." We knew a Texan had been before us.

As we drove further up we had to stop more frequently, and the culture changed as well. Whenever we stopped a crowd gathered. Here both men and women wore a type of sarong, cloth wrapped loosely from the waist down with nothing covering their tops. My husband, being a red blooded male was fascinated when these women pushed up against him with their exposed breasts. At one stop an older woman came up to me and touched my shorts and said something. She sounded angry or scandalized and I did not know why.

On our way back down we did not have to stop so frequently. It was dark when we finally arrived back at the hotel and we were hungry. As we came into the nearly deserted dining room, we joined a student from Florida who was on a grant to study the culture and habits of the Balinese. As we described our experiences, and Jim described the young woman who seemed to have a banana cut in half and stuck on her chest, I must have sounded slightly scandalized.

The student turned to me and said, "Madam, you violated all their mores and scandalized the people. A hill country, Balinese consider the legs private and to be covered at all times. I notice that you are wearing short shorts. Women would ride side saddle at all times and would consider it very ugly to spread their legs around a man's back as you said you did." Then he muttered almost under his breath, "That's how we get the term, 'Ugly Americans.'"

CHAPTER 24

Without exception everyone who reads this chapter ends up laughing uproariously. At a book review, the oral reader was laughing so hard, that we had to ask her to read it again. This story also reminds our family of a fact about Nana: Do not make her mad or belittle her work, or she will find a way to make you wish you had not.

Mr. Ito & I

Nomura Securities invited me to come to Japan as their guest. I had been writing articles about various financial institutions that together made up Wall Street. Nomura had several branches in major cities in the United States, but their origin and heavy concentration of offices was in Japan. They were the Merrill Lynch of Asia.

With the cooperation of the Dean in the School of Business, I found a week in March that was free for me to go. The manager of the Nomura office in L.A. took over the planning for my week in Japan. He must have been a superman himself, because the schedule he planned left little time for sleeping.

Oh well, I could sleep when I came home. My flight would depart L.A. at 8 p.m. and was scheduled to arrive at the Tokyo airport after a twenty-three hour lapse of time.

John Ito met me on arrival, and proudly announced that Nomura had assigned him to me 24/7. Ouch! I hoped that was a figure of speech and not a reality. He spoke passable English, but he was about six inches shorter than me and weighed not much more than my 123 lbs. I was beginning to feel like a giantess.

Mr. Ito said he was to take me anywhere I desired and "hang the expenses." Before I could say, "Take me to my hotel, and disappear for twelve hours," he whipped out a schedule and said that he was to take me to the Tokyo Stock Exchange for observation. Before I could get a word in edgewise he was plowing ahead, scattering people, and saying, "Make way! Make way for an important professor."

Embarrassed? Yes! But I decided to play his game, so I straightened my shoulders, held my head high, and looking neither to the left nor to the right, I plowed through the crowd. Mr. Ito hailed a taxi and bowed to me ceremoniously, ushered me into the back seat, then jumped in beside the driver. In five languages at least, he urged the driver to hurry, then in English, I heard "Hurry, hurry. She's late for a very important date." Oh no—he's read *Alice in Wonderland*.

On to the Tokyo Stock Exchange as scheduled! On two wheels and a prayer (mine) we traversed the twenty-five miles in record time. The taxi screeched to a stop, and before I could get my eyes open and my fingers unclenched, Mr. Ito had the door open and was pulling me out. As I reached for my purse and coat, Ito said "No, no, Ito get, you look!" He then spread his arms wide as if to embrace the entire imposing edifice of the Tokyo Stock Exchange. Thus began the strangest week of my life.

A New World

We hurried up the steps of the TSE, or rather I should say Ito hurried.

He would get three or four steps ahead of me, then turn back and offer me his arm. Since he was a head shorter than me, it made for an awkward connection.

Soon we were standing before an austere gentleman, and Mr. Ito was talking, gesturing, and pointing to me.

At last, we were admitted to an observation deck, and Ito rushed out saying that he was going to find an important broker. While he was away, I was able to relax and observe the action on the floor. I was amazed there was so much excited and noisy activity so late at night. The NYSE had limited hours of operation, from 9:30 to 3:30 EST. Evidently the TSE stayed open as long as there was a buyer and seller left standing on their feet.

I had thought the NYSE was a noisy place with each broker yelling out the terms of a transaction to his telephone clerk, but that didn't compare to the noise on the floor of the TSE. Here, each broker had two wooden blocks he clapped together to report the terms of a purchase or sale, and somewhere in this cavernous building someone or some machine heard and interpreted those claps. Unbelievable! I watched a broker who was clapping more often than most and I noted a certain cadence to his clapping. Perhaps that is how his clap is differentiated from all the rest.

Mr. Ito bounced back to the observation deck followed by the more sedate Mr. Huisui. In answer to my question, he explained the wooden blocks were called "claques" and each broker had his own claque, which was wired to a machine that recorded his order. When I expressed amazement at the rapid pace of claquing, Mr. Huisui said that sometimes a broker would overload his machine and suffer a lock-down, then have to leave the room for fifteen minutes while someone else would get his orders and commission. Sure enough, I looked down and my excited broker was gone and someone else was standing in his place.

When Mr. Huisui asked me what I wanted to do next, I told him I wanted to get some much needed sleep. He gave Ito instructions and Ito seemed disappointed that I wanted to cut the evening so short. Ito grabbed a taxi and we headed to the Imperial Hotel. He escorted me to my room and proudly showed me the beautiful bouquet and night cap that had been provided. I thanked him and gently edged him out and closed the door. I was afraid he might try to put me to bed. Ito has got to go!

As I undressed and did minimal preparation for bed, I remembered I was scheduled to spend the day at my host's office, and I would ask about another guide. As I crawled into a bed for the first time in over thirty-five hours, I heard a slight noise outside my door. Was Ito on watch?

* * *

When the bedside phone rang, I groaned and looked at my watch: 7:30 a.m. I answered groggily and heard Ito sing in falsetto voice, "Rise and shine for a very important day." I could have killed him, but instead I said very firmly that I would meet him at the admission desk in thirty minutes. I then added that I wanted a very substantial breakfast as I had eaten only airline food since leaving home.

About thirty minutes later, I opened my door and there stood Ito.

"Hurry, hurry, taxi waiting," he said.

I reluctantly entered the taxi, thinking about the breakfast I might have had in the hotel dining room.

We traveled over several streets and stopped at a small cafe advertising *Americanized Food*. After being seated with ceremony at a table set for one, a woman, smiling broadly, set before me a cereal bowl filled with corn flakes, a glass of milk, and a dish of fresh strawberries.

I smiled my thanks, but before I could begin to eat, a young lady entered with three waffles and a container of syrup. As she stepped back, a man entered with a platter filled with a huge steak and three eggs. He stepped back and began patting the air. I looked inquiringly at Ito who explained that Mr. Moggu was telling me this was the famous Kobe beef made tender by years of patting the cow.

Before I could think of anything to say for this honor, another older woman entered with a huge bowl of fresh fruit. They stood back, smiling, as Ito said, "Eat. Eat." Oh my, how had Ito explained my desire for a substantial breakfast to these good people? I ate a bit from each dish, then stood and rubbed my stomach to indicate that I was overfilled. It wasn't far from the truth, since my skirt felt two sizes too small.

The waiting taxi driver took us back to the financial area of downtown Tokyo, and I spotted a sign advertising the Far East Wall Street Journal. I wondered if it were printed in English. Ito said that it was and asked if I wanted one. When I answered in the affirmative, he gave instructions to the driver, who began an intricate and dangerous back tracking through the heavy traffic until he reached the Far East Building. Ito jumped out, ran into the building, and emerged minutes later, waving the paper in triumph above his head. That victory had been achieved at the near cost of life and limb—mine, if I was correctly interpreting the angry mutterings of the taxi cab driver.

Again, I resolved that Mr. Ito must go, but until then I had to be very careful about what I said.

When we arrived at the Nomura Securities building, Mr. Ito went in search of my contact. While he was gone, I asked the receptionist where I would find the officer who had assigned Ito as my guide.

She sighed and said, "Poor Mr. Ito."

When I demanded an explanation, she said that Ito was the nephew of Mr. Sunyat, the personnel director and he had promised his sister on her deathbed he would see that her son, John Ito, got a good job with the firm. He had failed several assignments, and Mr. Sunyat had said that if John Ito could not please a simple, unimportant, woman professor he was through.

A simple, unimportant woman? I decided to keep Ito and find some way to make Sunyat eat his words.

In my hotel room later that night, I wondered if I had reacted unwisely. Yes, I believed I had, but what was done was done, and I had to make the best of it.

While reading the Far East Wall Street Journal, I spotted an article titled *Observations from Abroad*. Interesting! Maybe, I had found a way.

High Praise

On the way to the Tokyo Stock Exchange the next morning, I told Ito I wanted to stop at the Far East building. Upon arrival, I started to get out and Ito began to insist that he would do everything that needed to be done, and for 24/7 the important professor wasn't to be bothered by anything. We finally compromised. He escorted me into the building, but he stayed outside the door while I talked to the editor.

The editor and I agreed that I would write three or four articles and he would publish them as soon as I could get them to him. I vowed to finish one each day so as to make a big impact. I also arranged to have a copy sent to Suilin, the receptionist, with instructions to include the copy in Sunyat's mail.

I had a very interesting and informative time at the TSE, but was anxious to get back to my hotel room, relax, and write my article. Later that afternoon at the hotel, Ito and I engaged in the same verbal battle: he wanted to help and I wanted to be alone. I won.

I ordered room service, put on comfortable clothes, and began to write. Words flew across the paper as I described the ingenious and unique wireless claque system used at the TSE. I finished by describing my first dramatic view of the Exchange and Ito's part in it. I then wrote "Mr. John Ito of Nomura, who showed such honor and respect, would make an extraordinary spokesman for the TSE."

The next day we went back to the Nomura office to observe the LP (low price) division in operation, and I noted that several employees smiled and wished Ito well. In the middle of my report on the day's observations, I wrote, "Mr. Ito's rapport with the other employees would make him a person of value in the Personnel Division." (Now, how do you like that, Mr. Sunyat?)

I had learned that day that Suilin was making copies of my articles, highlighting references about Ito, and including them in the mail of the six senior officers of the firm.

On Saturday we were scheduled to explore Tokyo and do a comparison with New York and the NYSE. Ito almost vibrated with excitement. He had worked and reworked the itinerary to show me as much as he could of his beloved Tokyo. We visited place after place after place until my feet cried out for mercy. I vetoed Ito's cure for sore feet: a communal bath with men and women together wearing no clothes.

That night in the hotel, with my feet in a basin of medicated hot water that my hotel maid said was "vely bueno," I reflected on the very many sights I had seen. It was difficult to pick one or two for my report.

I saw an ancient temple called the Geisha Girl Temple. With some diffidence, I asked how it had survived the massive bombing by our pilots during the war. Ito explained it had been completely destroyed, but had been rebuilt by the geisha girls (prostitutes) with their earnings from the occupying GIs. Then he added, "The Americans destroyed it and then the Americans built it back." He seemed to show no resentment against Americans for the atomic bombing of two of their cities, but only pride in the gleaming new buildings.

When I accepted the invitation to come to Japan, only about thirty-five years after the end of the war, I was wary of ill treatment. So far, I had not sensed any resentment; they were far too busy building a brand new world and becoming an economic power.

An activity I remembered with pleasure was stopping at a little hole-in-the-wall restaurant for a tempura feast. There were three vats of boiling oil surrounded by six stools on three sides of the vat. A chef stood on the fourth side with mounds of shrimp, other sea foods, and fresh, bite-size vegetables nearby. He would grab a piece of fish or vegetable with his chop sticks, coat it with the tempura paste or sauce, and then dip it in the hot oil for seconds. The chef worked at almost super-human speed because he would have another hot crisp morsel on your plate before you could finish the previous one. Yum, yum, they were good! (I took some of that tempura powder home, but it did not taste the same.)

I finished my report on my day in Tokyo by saying with true appreciation, "John Ito is a credit to Nomura Securities."

A Fond Goodbye

On Sunday morning, I invited Ito to watch "Hour of Power" hosted by Rev. Schuler with me in my hotel room. After all, I have been aware of the number of hours he had spent outside my door on what he called his

24/7 assignment. When the program—which had been translated into Japanese with English subtitles—ended, we went to a Buddhist Temple.

As per custom, we left our shoes at the door and I wondered how we would ever find them amid this sea of footwear. That wasn't a problem, and when we left I wanted to go back for more tempura, but the little restaurant was closed for Sunday.

A stroll through a very structured park was next on Ito's list. Later that night, after dinner and a much-too-short nap, I dressed more formally and we went to a Japanese opera, where men took and sang the women's roles. Ito explained what was happening on stage, much to the annoyance of other attendees, until even I was shushing him.

Monday's schedule called for a visit to some budding corporations.

We watched the assembly line at Toyota, and I compared it with the one I had seen at the Mercedes plant in Germany I had visited a couple of years earlier.

Both of them were more labor efficient than the ones in Detroit, but that's understandable. Their old, labor intensive factories were destroyed and rebuilt by a benevolent enemy.

The Toyota engineers were trying to develop gasless cars. More power to them. I made a mental memo to see if I could purchase some of their stock on the OTC back home.

We then visited the Itarin Corporation, a small company that was trying to develop computer games. I doubted that that company would be successful. (Ha! That company, under another name became "the darling of Wall Street.")

We revisited the restaurant where I had been offered such a huge breakfast, but this time I ordered from the menu. That night I wrote my last article for Observations, in which I thanked Nomura Securities for sponsoring my trip to Japan, and for furnishing such an informative guide as John Ito. The next morning, I left for the twenty-two hour trip back to California with Ito's voice ringing in my ears, "Hurry, hurry."

Weeks later I received a note from Suilin saying that Ito had been assigned to Mr. Sunyat, and he was slowly, but surely, driving Mr. Sunyat crazy. I could almost hear her giggling.

CHAPTER 25

As you read this interesting chapter, you will find out how Nana's extraordinary industriousness got her into serious trouble with the Board of Higher Education. Who would think you could do too much too efficiently. How did she explain her actions?

Double-Dipping . . . A No No

A recurrent refrain found in many of the chapters of this autobiography was "California, Here We Come" and described my family's plan to join the Post War migration to California—"the land of milk and honey" and economic opportunity. But, as you have observed, something always interfered—economic necessity, a too-good-to-pass-up job, The Ford Foundation Scholarship, and more. It wasn't until twenty years later that my family finally migrated to California.

One result of the post-war migration was that coastal land for development became very scarce and expensive. Developers flattened, terraced, or created land. But many builders though, turned their attention inland away from the coast. Orange grove and avocado grove owners received multiple offers to purchase their land. I had some of these "instant millionaires" as clients. One of my favorites was Mr. Ruis. Although he had just deposited $27,000,000 in the bank, he referred to himself as a dirt poor farmer and said, "I don't have one darn thing I want to buy." It was most frustrating. When I wanted to talk about stocks, bonds and options, he wanted to talk about the night he manned the smudge pots to protect his fruit. If I were ever to pin him down to make a decision about buying 1000 shares, he would tell me to buy it without bothering him. "I trust you," he said. Ouch!

Hard on the heels of the developers with their fat checks, were the con artists and the get-rich-quick operators. Mr. Ruis went back to Ohio to join his family.

He could not stand the sight of seeing row after row of prize orange trees cut down to make room for row after row of look-a-like houses.

Irvine Ranch was the largest parcel of undeveloped land in Orange County. Developers were salivating with desire over the Ranch. They wanted to make it available for homes, businesses, and more as the demand increased with the rapid inland expansion. However the titles to the Irvine Ranch were a legal nightmare. In the 1900s, Jim Irvine, an early pioneer, began buying up isolated land until he had accumulated around 1600 acres. He developed a rather unique method of financing his purchases. He left all the development rights with the seller and thus, bought the land for practically nothing. Those development rights were sold and resold, gambled away, or forgotten. In the following years, Irvine heirs sold parts of the Ranch and often such sales were not recorded. To complicate matters, a large entity in Mexico, backed by the government, claimed much of Southern California by way of a land grant from the King of Spain, when they claimed ownership of California. Eventually, using the power of eminent domain, the USA and Orange County took control of the Ranch and created the Irvine Foundation to devise an orderly plan for development and compensate owners if they could prove ownership.

Taxes had not been paid over the years by most owners, so Orange County levied a huge tax bill on the Ranch, which the Foundation paid by giving the University of California system over 200 acres of prime land. The purpose was to create the University at Irvine to serve the expected growth as the population moved inland. After months and years of hurried planning, large university buildings arose in the former cattle ranch. Soon supporting buildings, like dorms, fast food joints, book stores and faculty housing were built.

The buildings were up, the students were coming, but the administration was having trouble getting qualified faculty to come to this new, untested university in the middle of a cattle ranch. That fact led to my first, and last, confrontation with the university hierarchy. Perhaps you will remember that a full load for a full professor was nine units of class hours per week. I had been assigned to the graduate school, so most of my students were working on their Master's Degree. Most of them worked during the day and attended school at night. I scheduled my classes for Tuesday from 7 p.m. to 10 p.m. On Thursday, I came on campus at noon and held an office hour, a three hour afternoon class and a three-hour graduate class at night. Thus, I completed my nine hours of class work and office hour on Tuesday and Thursday. You may also remember that we had moved inland to be closer to the center of the new development, so I was closer to the UC IRVINE.

Gradually, Dr. Browning, the Dean of Scheduling, asked me to teach more classes at UCI extension division. I often ended up teaching a six-hour seminar or two three-hour classes for graduates who were working on advanced degrees on weekends or evenings. Then, in the summer term of 1972, I agreed to teach Investment Analysis for a professor on leave. That was a rather full load, but I didn't mind since I had agreed to teach at USC that summer. Many of the attendees were men I worked with on the Economic Development Council or had met at one or more social clubs when I had been the speaker.

Then disaster struck, or so it seemed to me. I received an official letter from the Provost Marshall's office commanding my appearance at a hearing investigating a matter of utmost concern. It also suggested that I bring an attorney with me. Every professor knows that the Provost Marshall is the disciplinary arm of the university system. His office is often referred to as the "whipping post." What had I done?

I frantically reviewed recent speeches and actions to find anything that had offended the administration. Then I learned the Deans from UCI and CSU had been summoned to that same hearing. We hired an attorney who learned that some payroll clerk spotted my name and pay as a full professor at USC and also UCI. Somehow, William Fuller, a political appointee heard about the double dipping and made it a "cause celeb." I was either cheating the schools big time, or professors were paid too much for too little work. He demanded a review of the entire payroll records and swore to either reduce salaries or increase hours worked. Wow! The full professors would hold me responsible if they lost the hard won nine-hour/full pay package! We put together a credible defense and went to the hearing.

My Dean at USC related that I was most in demand at the Speaker's Bureau, and that my activities brought more favorable honor to the school than anyone else. He further pointed out that unlike most profs, who were at the payroll window within hours of the delivery of the checks, I had not picked up my checks in four months. Therefore, I had not taken two pay checks from the university system. It was a technical point, but it saved the day. The Dean from UCI said that he scheduled me to teach in response to student demand.

As an example, he said that some brokers and dealers in the securities industry requested a seminar on recent legislation affecting their industry. Because of my wide exposure to the industry, he asked me to arrange a seminar. I held a very successful day with the Securities and Exchange Commission. Speakers from the SEC, NASDAQ, and even an Australian, who explained the Austrian equivalent of the Security and Exchange Commission, were scheduled.

The payroll clerk said that no other case of double dipping was found.

A respected full professor told of the number of hours he typically spent in class preparation, research, and writing. The Deans and I were acquitted of wrong doing and were praised for our service to the university.

The Marshall said to me, "Although it is obvious that you are a superwoman and can do well in two jobs at the same time, I must order you to work for only one university in our system." Looking at Mr. Fuller, the political appointee, he added that we must avoid any appearance of wrong-doing. I chose USC. However, within two years, I was back at Irvine. A group of sudden millionaires, who sold their orange groves to developers, created a Guest Lecture Series at Irvine and I was asked back as a guest lecturer.

CHAPTER 26

I only knew one person mentioned in this chapter, my Papa, Dr. JR Belt. He was a tall blue eyed gentle and jolly man. He was always making jokes and singing songs about liking to go swimming with "bow legged" women.

My grandparents tried to go camping every summer, and they often took me with them in "Mimi," a camper named after me. I have many wonderful memories, but one of my most memorable was of my "gold strike" in Idaho. Papa and I were inner-tubing down a river in a park in Idaho when I spotted something shiny shimmering in the water. Papa was quick to tell me that I had found gold and shouted, "Gold, gold, by golly you found gold!" I borrowed Nana's sieve and started collecting all the flakes I could find.

Soon I began dreaming of all the things I would buy with the gold.

I worked for and dreamed for nearly three hours until I had collected what I considered to be a fortune. That night we went to the camp fire, and despite my grandparents attempting to keep me blissfully ignorant, the park ranger informed me the gold I had found was merely pyrite or fool's gold, and effectively "burst my bubble." What a disappointment!

Independent Professional Women Also Need Men

In the 1950s I was, as far as I knew, the only woman in a man's world of finance. Their reaction to an unexpected woman in their midst formed the basis for many interesting experiences as I competed with men for space and opportunity. However, men played an important part in shaping my life and career. Here are just a few of them.

THOMAS MONROE MCKEMIE

My fraternal Grandfather McKemie stressed the importance of excellence in education. If it seemed that I might not make the top score (A) in any subject, like music, he would hire a tutor. He would often say, "You can be among the best and above the rest. It is up to you." Then he would add, "But I expect the best."

I was ten-years-old in 1933, the start of Roosevelt's economic plans to cure the Depression. Believing in self-reliance and "the less government, the better," Grandfather was no fan of Roosevelt's "alphabet soup" plans. I followed him around as he tried to run his business "in spite of that mad man in the White House." I came through my biased economic education with flying colors. Years later, when I earned my doctorate degree in economics, I then understood what my grandfather had taught.

GEORGE WASHINGTON LOUCKS

My maternal Grandfather Loucks fostered my public speaking activity. He was a deacon at our church, and was constantly lining up churches and clubs where I would go and recite a piece. One of my earliest memories was of him lifting me up on his big Germanic shoulders to recite a poem. I was three-years-old. Later he backed the WCTU (Women's Christian Temperance Union) because I was appearing every Saturday morning on their radio program, delivering speeches and urging the passage of prohibition. This called for some sacrifice because he did enjoy his pint in the evening. In my junior year in high school, I entered the Illinois Better Speaking Contest. As I advanced from local to county to district to sector and finally the state, he sat through each nail-biting contest until I won the title of Illinois' Best Speaker.

When I lost at the national level, he lamented that he should have gone with me. This early experience in public speaking enabled me to become the most popular person in the University Speakers Bureau. When I became a spokesman for the American Bankers Association, I said a short prayer of thanks to my Grandfather.

CHARLES FRANKLIN MCKEMIE

My beloved father, Charles (Charlie) Franklin McKemie, taught me, by example, how to "win friends and influence people" until he died in 1970.

Everyone who had the privilege of knowing him liked him. Again by example, he taught me to be industrious. Often, he would work two or three jobs at the same time.

For example, he might work the day shift at the mine, come home to milk the cows and feed the chickens, pigs and horses, and the many other chores that a well-run farm requires. Then at dusk, he would get the tractor out and go to mow the borders of the highways, as per his contract with the state.

Later that night, Mom would bundle up my baby sister and me and take a hot meal to Dad. While he ate under the star studded sky, we would enjoy some precious and quiet family time. He protected and cared for me for twenty years, and then, rather reluctantly, he turned me over to the care of James Radford Belt, my husband for fifty-three years, until he died on May 1, 1996.

JAMES RADFORD BELT

The Master of Ceremony was introducing me to the gathering of businessmen, to whom I was getting ready to speak, when the man on my right shocked me by whispering, "One must wonder what your husband is like. If you were my wife, you would be home, where you belong, having babies."

Before I could retort, the MC finished and I rose to polite applause. The reaction to my speech was gratifying and the Q and A was lively.

When I next looked, the chair of the rude macho male was empty.

What is your husband like? I would like to answer that question now. Jim was very handsome with almost perfect facial features. He was tall and well proportioned (a basketball star) with a proud military stance.

He passed his blond hair and blue eyes on to our daughter and her two daughters, so we had a trio of beautiful blonds.

I, on the other hand, have glossy black hair (it used to be) with brown eyes and a dark tan, even in the winter time. Sex was an important part of our marriage, but not overly important. Jim did love to hug and cuddle. When I was home, we went to bed early, but when he fell asleep and released his grip on me, I would slip out for two or three hours to prepare my lecture or speech for the next day.

Jim was very confident and knew his worth in our marriage. He had his own job, his own interests, his own business, just as I had mine. I believe that our marriage lasted fifty-three relatively harmonious years (in spite of the dire prediction that it would not last six months) because we were not under each other's feet all the time. We both recognized that Jim was the major bread earner. Making speeches and serving on government committees earned a lot of publicity and honor, but was mostly pro bono for me. Even the work for the American Bankers Association and the United Nations did little more than gain favorable publicity, and allowed me to see much of the world, all expenses paid.

Jim's real estate business allowed us to live in a million dollar house and entertain lavishly, although my creative financing played a big part. In fact, I like to think of myself as a co-partner in his real estate investment business. He would find the deals and ask me to "push the pencil" (do due diligence) to determine its financial soundness.

Jim was always very supportive. He would often fly me to professional meetings in his private plane, and, if possible, he accompanied me on writing several books and on overseas assignments. He did not feel threatened like the man who declared, "I would not marry you for all the tea in China. Within months, or even weeks, you would have completely destroyed my male ego." Although he would never say so, I like to think that Jim was proud of me.

DR. ROBERT MORRIS

Another man who enhanced my career was Dr. Robert Morris (name changed for discretion). He was a noted and much quoted professor at a famous and respected eastern university. He had published many books and articles. In fact, I had used two of his published theories in my classes. The fields of finance, economics, and business have many organizations and Dr. Morris was an officer of or belonged to most of them.

I do not remember when I first met him, but our paths crossed and he remembered me. I received a letter from AIF Investment, inviting me to be a discussant at a seminar on the Morris Theories chaired by the author himself.

Since I did not know a lot about his rather complicated theory, I studied like mad for the July meeting. I discovered two questionable assumptions that I felt might be open for discussion. I must have done a creditable job because Dr. Morris invited me to join him at luncheon for further discussion. After that, I began to receive further invitations to take part in other programs, and Dr. Morris was often somewhere in the background.

Even I, naive as I was, began to wonder if it was my skill alone that was responsible for my sudden popularity. However, the powers-that-be at the university began to take note, and were very pleased that one of their professors was so active. The administration set up a special fund to help defer my expenses whenever I was a participant at a professional meeting. They even arranged to have an instructor teach my class if I had to be away at a meeting.

The Institute for Quality Analysis asked me to serve as secretary for a year and I agreed. It would be another step forward in my career and enhance my credits with my bosses. The next IQA Journal announced my appointment to the Board, but also said that the Honorable R L Morris had agreed to serve as Chairman of the Board. It further stated the two new members would be introduced in May at the next IQA meeting in Chicago.

When I arrived at the hotel for the May meeting of IQA, I found not only the key to my room, but a note from Dr. Morris asking me to join him at the night club to hear Robert Goulet. If I agreed, a taxi would arrive at 9:45 p.m.

From the moment I arrived at the Club, I felt like a celebrity. Our table was front and center, and we had our own personal wine steward. Robert Goulet even left the stage and came to our table. He held my hand and sang a love song. Oh, wow!

When the concert ended, most diners left, the lights were turned down low, soft music filled the room and we talked. Dr. Robert (call me Bob) Morris said he had become fascinated by the woman who was breaking all the rules of male dominance in the field of business. He believed that with his sponsorship, I could go further and faster. Bob said that he had long wanted to find a special companion who spoke his language, and could help relieve his boredom at the many meetings he was required to attend.

After setting up some guidelines—no sex, discretion at all times, share of expenses, etc.—the strangest long distance relationship was born. Bob was fifteen to twenty years older than I, and a few inches taller. He was not as handsome as my Jim. Bob honored and respected his wife and was proud of his two sons, so we agreed on a partnership of sorts.

Upon my return to California and resumption of my duties at CSU, I began to wonder what, if anything, would happen next. The whole episode seemed unreal. Then I had a horrible thought. What if it were some cruel hoax, engineered by men to give a woman, who thought she was as good as a man, her "comeuppance." No! Then, the letters began to arrive, usually two a week, in envelopes with return labels from different associations. They contained items of interest, questions for the next telephone call, or small gifts.

About a month after the IQA meeting, the program director for the Money Today Group invited me to submit a paper for publication in MONEY and attend a follow up discussion at the meeting in August. Upon acceptance, details would be sent. What a coup!

Bob's letters and calls during the next month contained ideas for my paper. I wrote and rewrote it a dozen times. When my paper was accepted for publication, the official announcement arrived with one change; the date allowed me one extra day and night at the hotel. It also contained a travel voucher to cover the cost of changing my schedule.

The hour for my performance arrived and I was charged up. A speaker can always tell when they have the audience with them in full approval. I did!

Bob, standing in the background, seemed to enjoy my praises as much as I did.

The next day Bob hired a car and we drove north following the shores of Lake Michigan. A sign pointing toward the Great Lakes Navy base triggered my memories of the early years of married life spent there, and I told Bob about my past. He then shared some memories of his early years with me.

This further cemented the details and expectations of this strange, long term and long distance relationship between a male professor from the northeast and a woman professor from the southwest. But we were both careful to honor our marriage vows, and agreed that if anything threatened either one, we would cease all contact immediately.

As planned, once a month on average, I would be invited to participate in some professional meeting. If I agreed, I would be sent an official announcement of time, place, and stipends. The dates would be altered to give me an extra day or two. Even though we described our meetings as platonic, he did love to hug and cuddle. I soon learned not to have my hair set before I left home. Bob liked my hair "soft and smelling of my coconut shampoo."

Even though Bob was responsible for my early invitations, my performances resulted in invitations on my own. Several times I had to turn down an altered date because I had accepted another professional group's invitation.

The campus post office became used to receiving mail for me from many different organizations. Bob wrote twice a week, using the stationary of groups to which he belonged. He wrote about the latest IPO or some stock recommendation; he disputed some recently published theories or some government action. It was like getting a private education from a prominent teacher.

Often the letter contained a small piece of jewelry, such as a pearl for the necklace we were building. Pearl is the jewel for June. I am a Gemini, born on June 6th. If he wanted to write something personal, he did it in shorthand. I had taken shorthand for only one semester in high school all those many years ago so I needed a shorthand book, but because that is an ancient form of communication I could not find one. I had to admit that I had misstated when I told him I knew shorthand.

Whenever possible, Bob called during my office hours. We talked about the latest happenings in the world, in our lives, grants I was trying to get, honors he had received. We kept it short and general so that if anyone overheard, it was just two professors discussing current events. Thinking of novel ways to communicate added spice to the relationship. Secrecy provided a hint of naughtiness when there was nothing naughty about it.

We began to meet less frequently since Bob was attending fewer of the professional meetings because of his declining health. Seven years after our first discussion, a wrapped package arrived. It contained a copy of the latest IQA Journal. On the black bordered cover was a picture of Dr. Robert Morris and the words *In Memoriam*. Bob must have confided in someone so that I would know why our relationship had come to an end. I mourned in silence for my friend, my teacher, and my sponsor.

CHAPTER 27

My cousin, Danielle, and her husband in the diplomatic corps spent three years in Thailand on assignment. Her enthusiastic description of Thailand along with Nana's description made Thailand high on my list of must see places. But Nana's experiences in Thailand were special, as you will see.

Financial Lady — Oriental Style

For three weeks during the Christmas season, 1981, I lost my identity.

No, it wasn't because of "identity theft"; it was Mr. Limtanacool's way of taking me to all male gatherings. He would press his palms together, fingers pointing toward his chin, a typical Thai greeting, bow his head and say, "Meet my financial lady." Thus, I became known as financial lady, not Dr. McKemie-Belt. But I'm getting ahead of myself.

I had known that in some societies, there was a division between men and women. At a dinner at the Limtanacool home in California, I was the only woman at the table, although I could hear women's laughter coming from another part of the house. Why then, had a woman such as I, been invited to be the guest of one of the wealthiest and most influential men in Thailand?

Later, Mr. Limtanacool himself explained. He had sent several sons, sons-in-law, and junior employees to CSU, and most of them had taken my class in International Finance. When they came back he began to hear statements such as, "Dr. Belt said this and she said that," or "Dr. McKemie said this and that."

"Since most of what you said seemed sensible to me," he told me, "I wondered if you would come to Thailand and give me your input on two vexing problems we have. I told my son-in-law, Lon Julicon, to negotiate with you. He suggested late December when the lower humidity made our hot, humid climate more bearable by others, and that you would be on the Christmas vacation." Lon left for CSU with instructions to try for three weeks.

My first reaction to Lon's offer was that I did not want to be away from home during Christmas, but after talking to the family and realizing this was a once-in-a-lifetime opportunity, I agreed. The financial terms were quickly set and we began work on the airline scheduling. This was complicated because Mr. Limtanacool (call me "Mr. Lim") kept changing the places he wanted us to visit. Lon became overwhelmed with instructions and counter instructions such as, "If the supplier agrees, go to Guam, but if he doesn't agree, skip Guam and go to Taiwan . . . No, go straight to Japan!"

Finally Mr. Lim told Lon he would come to CSU and we would wing it.

Within hours after his arrival, he upgraded my flight to first class and we were off.

If you have never traveled Japanese first class, you have not enjoyed the best. I observed another thing that made me slightly ashamed. His expensive luggage, a la Deck, was examined very, very carefully at both the L.A. and Hawaiian checkouts while mine, a la Target was barely looked at.

We spent an overnight in Hawaii, and made a profitable deal with a supplier the next day. I made a suggestion in my host's favor, which was adopted. I felt that I had earned my airfare upgrade. After flying most of the night, then sleeping a few hours in the Taipei Hotel, we set out for another meeting. It was then that I was introduced as my "financial lady."

On the way to the meeting, I saw something that would never happen in America. Hordes of people were looking at a board that was half a block long. I asked aloud what they were looking at. A Taiwanese lawyer, who had joined us for the meeting, explained the mid-term grades from the twenty-two high schools in Taipei, the capital of Taiwan, had been posted on that board.

The people were looking not only for the grades of their own, but for the grades of children of neighbors, friends, partners, competitors, or even enemies.

* * *

The meeting I attended was conducted mostly in Mandarin between lawyers, and it left me time to wonder what the United States, which had signed a peace treaty with Taiwan, would do if Communist China decided to take back the small capitalistic democracy. God forbid! Maybe China would become more capitalistic itself and covet Taiwan less, as they considered Taiwan's financial success an irritant and a bad example to their own impoverished people.

After a late luncheon with Mr. Limtan, third brother to Mr. Limtanacool, we left for Japan. I learned that the two mainland Chinese people aboard the plane had come to Taiwan because the Chinese have a long memory of the brutal invasion of China by Japan before World War II, and they forbade anything from Japan, especially its airplanes, on Chinese soil.

When we arrived at the hotel, Mr. Lim went to his room after telling Lon to take me anywhere I wanted to go. Since we were both tired, we decided to have a light supper at the hotel, and over our last cup of tea, I told him about my previous visit to Tokyo. We laughed at my adventures or misadventures with Mr. Ito. (See Chapter 24 – Mr. Ito and I)

An Exquisite Lifestyle

We were scheduled to meet some buyers of marble from the Limtanacool Mines in SE Thailand. We were to meet for brunch at a noted Japanese restaurant that was known for its adherence to Japanese culture.

Upon our arrival, the surprised men were introduced to "my financial lady," and we entered a private room that had been reserved for us. In typical Japanese fashion, we left our shoes in the care of an attendant, and were then seated on a pillow by a very low table (about nine inches off the floor).

I soon realized that I had made an error in my choice of attire that morning: a yellow business suit with a very tight skirt with a tight, above knees hem line. The tight skirt left me no room to maneuver, so I folded my legs under me and sat on them. By the end of the first hour, I could no longer concentrate on the discussion. I could think only of my discomfort and hope the meeting would end soon. After two hours, I could not feel my legs. At the two-and-a-half-hour mark the meeting seemed to be breaking up, and I whispered to Lon to help me get up for fear I would topple over, face forward onto the table and embarrass everyone. Fortunately, I was able to stand, with help, and we hurried to the airport.

*   *   *

Our arrival at the Bangkok airport was eye-popping. Two extended Mercedes pulled up as soon as the plane stopped, with flags flying indicating VIP status, and some cloth covered steps came out of the plane as Mr. Limtanacool and I descended. As we entered the car, the steps receded and the other passengers left through the terminal.

As we traveled, Mr. Lim explained about the compound where I would be living, unless I preferred to go to a hotel. He and his wife lived in the original home, and as each child married a new modern home was built. At present there were six newer homes in the compound with three children still living at home.

At our approach, the massive gates of the walled compound were opened by two Thai, who gave my host the traditional greeting, palms pressed together, fingers pointing to the chin with head bowed. In the Old House, an attractive woman, wearing a beautiful silk dress cut on very slim lines with slits on each side to allow for easy movement, came into the room and gave Mr. Lim the traditional greeting, which he returned.

No hugging, kissing, or even touching, which was considered very bad form.

He introduced his wife who graciously welcomed me. She spoke limited English, but a maid who was with her at all times, interpreted for her.

She explained that Quilee would be my maid, and a pretty Thai girl with dark hair and snapping black eyes came forward.

Soon men entered the room, each giving the respectful greeting to Mr. and Mrs. Limtanacool first, and then greeted me. Three of the men and Lon were former students, and each seemed eager to tell me what they had been doing since I had last seen them.

Mrs. Lim left the room, and soon the men began to sit for the evening meal. I was seated on Mr. Lim's right and Lon to my right. The dinner conversation was conducted in English, which I believe was in deference to me, because it seemed formal and stilted, not free and easy as it would have been in Thai.

I learned some strange, interesting, and slightly disconcerting facts that evening. Each male guest had a Thai servant who made repeated trips to the kitchen to get more food or drinks, or just stood patiently waiting for orders. My maid stood behind my chair all evening, and I felt uncomfortable sitting and eating while she stood and waited. The windows were open and unscreened and I noted insects crawling on the ceiling of the dining room. Since our food was diced and highly spiced, I wondered if some of those insects had fallen into it. One of the things I remember most was the heat and humidity.

Even though it was December, the coolest month of the year, I hurried from one air conditioned room to another while I was there. Most of the men and even their servants were in short sleeved, white cotton shirts. Only Mr. Lim, Lon, and I were in suits. My lightweight yellow suit was making me feel like a wilted daffodil.

When Mr. Lim left, Lon, sensing my discomfort, escorted me to his home, which was air conditioned. There I met Barb, the oldest and very attractive daughter dressed in a beautiful Thai silk gown. When Barb and her husband Lon met, they bowed to each other in the traditional greeting: no hugging, kissing, or even touching, even though they had been apart for six months.

Very soon, a standard routine was established. During the weekdays, I traveled with Mr. Limtanacool to several points of interest where he had business connections and where many business conferences were held. I was the only woman at such meetings, and I was always introduced with the traditional bow and the words "meet my financial lady." It seemed to me, the meetings were polite ceremonies and not much was accomplished, but Lon explained that Oriental business was done that way. The principals would meet first, then the assistants would meet to do the real bargaining. Each would have instructions gained at that first meeting: i.e. that man is anxious to do the deal, but that one is indifferent, so bargain accordingly. I have heard many Americans express frustration when dealing with Orientals, and I now understood why.

During the evenings and on weekends, a member of the family would escort me to all the must-see places or events, such as the huge gold Buddha, the royal barge, many temples, the farmer's boat market, plays, entertainments and schools. Before I left Thailand, I did everything on the must-do list but ride an elephant.

*　　*　　*

While we were dining at the Limtan Soap Factory, Mr. Lim related his experiences during the Communist Revolution. He was the third son of a wealthy Chinese family. His father, fearing the Communists would overrun their inland province, decided to send his sons out of China while he still could. His eldest son had already escaped with the Loyalist and Chiang Kai-shek to Taiwan. One son went to Hong Kong, another went to Burma, and Mr. Lim went to Thailand. He grew quiet and reflective for a moment, and I asked if he knew what had happened to his parents. He shook his head and said sadly that the last time he had heard, they were living under house arrest and were to be tried by a people's court.

When Mr. Lim, his wife, and two sons arrived, they expanded the factory until they had a Proctor & Gamble like plant with many extensions, ranging from a marble mine in the south to a brewery in the north with varied types of businesses in between.

Although Mr. Lim, was increasingly being asked to arrange a private meeting between business associates and the "financial lady," I knew the major reason I was in Thailand was to help Mr. Lim solve his business problems. I was beginning to sense the source of the problem that even Mr. Lim didn't recognize.

Fifty years after his arrival, Mr. Lim, at age seventy-five, was still trying to do hands-on management of all these varied businesses. I wanted to suggest that he divide his estate into five parts and distribute each to a trusted son or daughter, and then take a hands-off approach. Dare I do so? What would be his reaction? I know it is difficult for someone who has created an estate to give up control, even to the ones for whom it was created, before poor health or age force the transition. I decided to think about the idea for a while and I kept making hints; perhaps he'd get the idea himself. It's always best if a client thinks your idea is his.

Branching Out

As we flew to Chiang Mai—a city in North Thailand located on the famed Marco Polo trail that was the conduit in ancient times for commerce between the east and the west—Mr. Limtanacool explained his purchase and his problems with the brewery. Ten years ago, he had purchased it dirt cheap because it had several acres of land that he hoped to develop, but hadn't because of lack of time. The brewery had not made a clear profit yet, and he was looking for a way to dispose of it without too much loss. He hoped I could help him solve that problem. Oh wow!

I pressed him for financial details, and he pulled a jumbled bunch of papers from his brief case. He then said he was tired and would sleep while I studied the papers. Oh wow, again! I quickly said that he needed to have someone else handle the brewery so he could concentrate on more important matters. He mumbled sleepily and drifted off. I thought, maybe his mind would keep repeating my words as he slept.

After a few minutes of complete bewilderment, I went in search of Lon, who explained the figures were a mixture of Chinese, Thai, and English.

Before we landed, we had put together a rough statement of profit and loss.

With the addition of depreciation to an already sizable loss, Mr. Lim had a much bigger problem than he thought.

I asked Lon about the management of the brewery and learned that Frank Tuetye was a distant cousin of Mrs. Limtanacool. Frank had been away from the family compound and had thus escaped the slaughter of his entire family when the Communist army had swept through the area, killing everyone who had dared to oppose them. Eventually he had reached Thailand with reports on the fate of both families.

During the twenty-five mile trip from the Chung Mai airport and the brewery, Frank Tuetye cited a litany of woes, a mixture of mea culpa, and a whined, "It isn't my fault." Established customers were reducing their orders every year. The location near Chung Mai was an advantage during the camel pack or truck days, but now planes and trains carried most of the east to west commerce. The cost of ingredients was increasing yearly.

When we arrived at the brewery, I noticed acres of weed-covered land surrounding the brewery, giving it an unkempt appearance. Inside, less than half of the space was being used. We went into the tasting room and Frank seemed to come alive as he excitedly explained he had been experimenting with ingredients and had developed five different whiskeys. He wanted us to taste them and select the best. Since I did not like Scotch or any hard liquor, I suggested an alternative: a scotch tasting contest among local drinkers with generous prizes, to select the one Scotch that would become the ancient label of Limtan Scotch. Then the brewery could devise a unique bottle and double the advertising budget. I also suggested doubling the price of the scotch, justifying it with ads stating, "Not just any old scotch." Then I told them a salmon marketing story.

Salmon fishermen were catching more red salmon, but couldn't sell it or even give it away, because the people were used to the pale white color.

Some canny fisherman doubled the price of the red and advertised "A rich, robust taste, not like its pale imitation." Red salmon still sells for twice the amount of white.

I then asked about Chiang Mai—the population, average income, education, and more. If Chiang Mai was no longer an advantage, it might become an outlet for the brewery products. Frank was not well informed, but Con, who worked in the warehouse and had been assigned to make the visitors comfortable, did know. I questioned Con until I learned that it was a rapidly growing city. With Mr. Lim's permission, I then directed Con to arrange a meeting with the city fathers or elders, who could tell us about the city and surrounding areas.

I next turned my attention to the empty land and building. If I remembered my geography correctly, you could draw a line around the globe connecting Chiang Mai with Italy, France, and northern California, all wine producing areas. I wondered if wine grapes could be planted on the empty land. Then Lon spoke up and said there were several small grape growers in the surrounding countryside. Lon, Con, and I spent most of the night studying different plans for saving the brewery. By morning, we had a plan ready to present to Mr. Lim.

There were two parts to the plan, and the first concerned the brewery.

We proposed retaining the brewery at a much reduced size, and just one product, Scotch. Con would be responsible for changing the existing marketing, allowing the company to put the scotch in every pub, liquor shop, or grocery store in Chiang Mai and the surrounding areas. We proposed buying the most prominent shelf space in stores available. Currently only one shop carried the scotch, which was placed way back. Brochures would be distributed wherever the scotch was sold proclaiming a worldwide search was being made to identify the scotch that is good enough to carry the famous label, *Limtang*. "Watch this space; soon the good citizens of Chiang Mai will be invited to join the taste-testing party."

The second part of the plan called for the creation of a winery as the best and most profitable use of the weed choked land and unused space inside the brewery. Lon then explained that during any free time he had while he was working on his MBA, he had traveled to the vineyards in central and northern California, going from one wine tasting party to another. He took Thais or other Asians with him, and discovered by observation the preference was for wine made from the Pinot grapes. From a contact he had made on his last trip to Chiang Mai, Lon had learned there was a small vineyard about seventy-five miles from the brewery where they grew Pinot.

According to rumor, the owner had two assets that would enable us to get into the winery business quickly—he had thousands of bottles of aged, chilled wine in his warehouse and a nursery of Pinot grapes ready for planting.

I wanted the management to go to the vineyard the next day and bargain for the wine and plants. Mr. Lim agreed, but looked slightly worried as if things were moving too fast. Frank was looking alarmed, who would do all the work?

To make the plan work, I had to make two other proposals. Lon and Con thought I was stepping into a hornets' nest. Perhaps I was, but I needed to try. I proposed the family establish a five-year, 75,000 Baht revolving credit line to provide seed capital for the new business. We worked out a tentative budget that showed it could be paid off in three years. Mr. Lim looked shell shocked, and I steeled myself for his response to my next proposal.

Every business, and especially this one, needs the best hands-on management it could get. I, therefore, proposed that Mr. Lim sell the brewery to his daughter, Bard and Lon, her extremely talented husband, for 1 baht.

They could then move to Chiang Mai to provide the much needed hands-on management for the new winery project.

"Barb would never agree to move to Chiang Mai," sputtered Mr. Lim.

Lon spoke up and asked for permission to present his wife's case.

A Quandary

Three months ago they had found a magnificent mansion for sale and Barb wanted to use her trust fund to buy it. The Thai-style mansion was well maintained and very little modification was needed to make it Barb's absolute dream house. The living quarters and seven bedrooms upstairs would provide luxury for Barb and any Limtanacool who wished to visit. She planned to create an exclusive and expensive Limtan House, which would become *the* place to go. The mansion contained three large rooms that opened from the lakeside veranda.

The first room would be the Tea-House for women. It would feature the finest of linen and Spode china, and serve the finest of Oriental spiced tea and finger sandwiches. She believed that women's clubs and church or business groups would come often to splurge at her tea house. Also, affluent women in groups of three or four would come for tea and gossip.

From 5 until 7 p.m., the second room would be open to businessmen for a before-dinner drink of Frank's best Scotch. The businessman and his company would be announced as he entered. The Scotch House would hopefully become known as the place where deals are made.

At 8 p.m. the House of Fine Wines would open for couples in formal dress. Beside a small table for two, a Wine Steward, dressed in a tuxedo, would have a bottle of the finest wine chilled in a quality ice bucket. He would open the bottle with great ceremony and urge the businessman to do the sniff-and-sip test before he pours the wine. There would also be a band and a small dance floor. The rooms would be by reservation only and Barb hoped these would have to be made weeks in advance; exclusivity is like cat nip to the wealthy.

"Barb begs you to go and see the house, Mr. Lim," Lon said. "It is by far the most spectacular house you will ever see."

Mr. Lim grunted in response. Too much had been proposed. We could only hope he could sort it out before we had to leave. I also hoped he would realize that I have not only kept him from losing his shirt on the disposition of the money-losing brewery, but I had found a new source of income and brought honor to the Limtang name.

New Plans

On the seventy-five mile trip to the vineyard, I was pleased to hear Mr. Lim ask Lon what he would do if he got the brewery, because that meant he was seriously considering our plan. Lon gave a very credible reply and shifted the conversation to his hopes for the winery and stressed that much depended on our success that day. The growers bottled more wine each month than he could get to market over bad roads with limited resources.

Following my idea, Lon urged Mr. Lim to offer forty percent of the wholesale price. If we found that all of it was good, Mr. Lim would then pay wholesale price for all wine the owner could produce in the following years.

This offer would also be extended for cuttings in the nursery.

After spending a pleasant three hours with the vineyard owner, Mr. Suija, and learning all that we could about the storage of wine and planting a grape field, we started the three-hour trip back to Chung Mai. Mr. Lim was pleased because he had bought the wine for thirty-five percent of wholesale, citing cost of breakage on the bad roads. He ordered Con to waste no time in hiring transport for the wine and plants. Lon was happy because we had selected at random enough wine to fill both cars to capacity. He was anxious to prove that his choice of wine was correct.

I said dreamily, "Imagine the brewery this summer with a field of young grape plants fronting it on either side of a vine covered arched drive. A touch up of paint on windows and doors would accent the beauty of the weathered boards of the brewery. I believe it could become a destination drive for wine tasting or a 'wee dram' of Scotch." Frank, wearing his white lab coat, could supervise that. What do you think?"

Mr. Lim replied, "I can imagine it. Now, *you* make it happen."
Ouch!

We were scheduled to leave in two days and there was much to be done. I had to hire a painter and show him my vision. Farmers were needed to make the ground ready for planting the grape vines before the monsoons start.

I had also hoped that Con could convince Mr. Suija to help him supervise the planting.

The next day, Mr. Lim, Lon, and I spent a very valuable half day with the city fathers of Chung Mai. He introduced me as the "financial lady" and Lon as the owner of the brewery. Wow, we were in! We were also given several concessions, including widening the quarter mile of road to the brewery. Mr. Lim would pay for permits (bribes) as a necessary part of doing business in the Orient.

That afternoon, Mr. Lim opened a line of credit in the National Bank of Thailand, then we visited the house Barb wanted to buy. It was spectacular beyond description. Even the inscrutable Mr. Lim was impressed. In the evening, we flew back to Bangkok while Lon stayed behind to become the boss of a project-in-progress.

Precious Gifts

We had only two days to get ready for our flight to Hong Kong. My clothes were cleaned, pressed, and repacked. In the morning, a tailor came for a final hem measurement for a famous Hong Kong suit. Before I went to Chung Mai, I was measured for the suit that no one should leave Hong Kong without. I had heard it could cost up to just several hundred dollars, but when I started to protest that I couldn't afford one, Barb made a gesture that meant "not to worry," but I did.

Mr. Lim spent half a day with Barb. I was not privy to that conversation, but she did not seem unhappy. Then he and Mrs. Limtanacool spent the last day with their sons, Lek and Ju. Lek was a senior at CSU and would fly back with me to graduate and start his MBA. Ju was the youngest son and would be a high school student and the adopted son of Jim and me. As usual, there was political unrest in countries nearby and Mr. Lim, ever cautious, felt he needed a son who was an American citizen, just in case. Lek and Ju would live in one of our condos near the campus.

We received a rousing welcome when we landed at the Hong Kong airport. Men, women, and children arriving in several cars were there to greet their uncle and cousins from Thailand. Our host, Mr. Jakkelee (call me Jack) was Mr. Lim's brother, and had been sent out of China ahead of the Communists' army to Hong Kong to save the family's iron-works business.

The business and his family had grown prodigiously. Jack, a big bear of a man with iron gray hair, said in a booming voice that he had "three wives and seventeen children."

During the evening, after a reception at the hotel, the men and I, at the invitation of Mr. Jack, filed into the dining room. There, on a table set with more gold trimmed items than I had ever seen before were lavish trays, containing three roasted whole pigs with the traditional apples in their mouths.

My mouth watered for a solid piece of that pork, but it was not to be. After personally feeding me pieces of pig skin with his "gold" chop sticks, Jack had the pigs taken away, and a clear soup with something floating in it was served next. He said it was shark fin soup and was very expensive. I wondered how I was going to eat it with chop sticks. He deftly broke off a piece of the fin and again fed it to me with his gold chop sticks. Then he picked up his bowl and drained it. He smacked his lips, encouraging me to do the same. Was he having fun at my expense? No, others were draining their bowls in the same way. Then the pork came back in bite size pieces, mixed with noodles, vegetables, nuts, and other ingredients that I couldn't recognize. It was good, but I still missed a big slice of pork.

The next morning, I was to "be suited" by Jack's wife, Suisue. The suit fitted perfectly, and I was very happy until I looked at the sales slip and saw $1,125, with a big dollar sign. Was it Hong Kong or American dollars? I tried to think of the exchange rate. Whatever, it was far more than I wanted to pay for any suit, especially a linen one that said dry clean only. I breathed a sigh of relief when the tailor took the slip and stamped it "paid in full."

Mr. Limtanacool and Jack took Lek, Ju, and me to the airport that evening. Mr. Lim was talking earnestly with his sons, when he suddenly hugged Ju. That was the first sign of affection I had seen between Thai's. He had given his youngest son to me and wouldn't see him again for six years.

Then he turned to bid me farewell. When I started to thank him for the suit, he waved my words away and said simply, "I am well pleased."

Postscript

One of Mr. Limtanacool's sons, Lek, became the chairman of the finance department of the University at Bangkok and invited me to come for a six week lecture tour.

One weekend we went back to Chiang Mai, and I was pleased to learn that both the brewery and Barb's mansion were popular destination points.

CHAPTER 28

The title of this chapter reminded me of a story Nana used to tell.

She said that at the beginning of the semester, Asiatic students stood when she entered; however she regretted that after a few weeks they would remain seated just as the Americans did.

To Stand or Not to Stand

I was pondering the question, *How did I get from there, a small mining and farming community in Southern Illinois, to here, thousands of miles above the Pacific Ocean?* on my way to Singapore to speak at the Asiatic Currency Unit meeting. My introspection had been triggered by James Beacon, who asked for an interview in Singapore, and said he hoped to get the answer to that question.

James was a reporter for United Press and was covering the ACU meeting. He was surprised and intrigued to learn the luncheon speaker, Dr. V. McKemie-Belt, was a female professor from California. Using the "Who's Who" publications, he found me in "A Thousand Women of the World" and strangely enough in "American Men of Science."

James found out I was born and grew up in Benton, Illinois, that I was married with one child, that I received the PhD degree from the University of Illinois, and that I was a professor at California State University. It was a large, internationally oriented college, but lacked the prestige of a Stanford or a Wharton or a Harvard. He had a list of my publications and of memberships in professional organizations, the typical biographic information. He said he was also a freelance reporter, and believed my stories of advancing in a man's world of money and banking would make a saleable human interest article.

He asked me to relate events or decisions that shaped my career as I moved from there to here.

As the hours and the miles rolled by, I thought of the milestones in my life, and wondered which ones James would consider of human interest and not just biographical. Perhaps, he would be interested in my first encounter with the banking system when I was ten-years-old. That was when I learned that I had lost all of my saving (all $28). Over the years, I had saved most of the silver dollars my grandfather had given me on birthdays, Christmas, and on special occasions when I pleased him with good grades. I had also saved most of my allowance and I had learned about the power of earning interest.

When I loaned to a friend, even my sister, a penny, I demanded two pennies in return.

Another interesting thing was my encounter with my history professor. When I asked him for a reference he said, "I had to give you an "A" because you earned it, but I *don't* have to give you a reference." He also said that I would never make a good historian because I was in too much of a hurry and looked to the future instead of the past. In a huff, I stormed across campus and changed my major to Business. The last semester I had taken an elective course in Money and Banking. It was the most interesting course I had ever taken and I learned what happened to my $28, so many years ago during President Roosevelt's "Bank Holiday." I deeply resented that history professor then for his "put down," but I bless him today.

Years later as a professor at Millikin University and an officer of the Illinois Finance Society, I dined with some members of the public relation's division of the Federal Reserve Bank in Chicago. I mentioned how frequently I used information from their Bulletin in my class work. A year or two later, the bank held a four-day seminar for college professors and CFOs from the five Midwestern states within their district, and I was invited to attend. During one of the sessions, the publicity department had arranged a group photo shoot and the resulting photograph showed thirty-nine men and one lone woman, front and center, me. This photo was published in the Bulletins of all twelve Federal Reserve Districts.

I recalled that a staff member of Ralph Edward's TV program "This Is Your Life" saw it and thought I would make an interesting and unusual story.

Most of the people featured on the program were celebrities, but occasionally they would feature someone simply because they led an interesting life.

A script writer and a camera man came to my home in Decatur and asked me to review all of the places I had been and what I had done there, which was easy to do, since talking about my life was one of my favorite topics. During the next two hectic weeks, they visited places I had talked about, gathered reams of material, and returned with a script they had me practice until they were satisfied. I had watched the TV show many times, assuming it was shot live in the NY studio. In my case, at least, it wasn't.

About a month later, I sat in my living room in Decatur and saw myself talking to the host, Ralph Edwards, and chuckled at the great surprise I showed when my fifth grade teacher walked in. She told about an incident I had almost forgotten:

"During a class assignment about what the student wanted to do or be when he or she grew up, most girls said a teacher or a nurse or get married or be a movie star. But not Virginia. She said that she wanted to pay income taxes and be in Who's Who."

Only three people in our whole county were rich enough to pay taxes during the Great Depression. Needless to say, I paid taxes long before I got into Who's Who. Thus, it seemed, I wished for fame and fortune.

*   *   *

After a stewardess took my drink and food order, I continued reminiscing. I recalled how for twenty years Jim and I had tried to go to California, and how I finally joined the staff of CSU, where I was employed for twenty-five years. I practiced grantsmanship and earned many trips to islands to study alternative energy for the United Nations.

One trip held particularly fond memories for me. I had managed to secure all-expense paid trips for twenty-five of my best students to visit the NYSE and other financial institutions in New York. The story, with pictures, was syndicated. The resulting publicity pleased the CSU administration very much. I chuckled as I thought about the note I received from the President of the University which read, "You have received more coverage from 'The Register' than all the press releases from the university for the past year, and that story has more value to the university than all the rest. Congratulations."

Finally, I thought that Mr. Beacon would be most interested to learn why the American Bankers Association, when asked to supply a luncheon speaker for the Asiatic Currency Unit's annual meeting, decided to send me. I signed up for the Speaker's Bureau, and several bankers asked for me to be their keynote speaker at annual, social and special financial meetings.

For the first time in the man's world of business, it paid to be a woman. There was a big push on to provide "Equal Employment Opportunity" or (EEO). Legislation and government procurement rules required that corporations prove they offered equal opportunities to minorities, including women. There was a severe shortage of qualified women in business, so I was asked to serve on several previously all-male boards and commissions.

I chuckled again as I thought about how I came to attention of the Union Bank in Los Angeles. They needed a token minority for their Board.

They persuaded an older board member to retire and appointed me to serve out his term, thus they became politically correct. Months later, the Public Relations division of the Union Bank put on a rather large production called "The Bank and the Community," to which political and business leaders were invited. I, representing the Board, was assigned a fifteen-minute segment just before lunch. I was preceded by officers of the bank, including the President and the CFO. I knew their speeches would have a certain amount of bravado and a lot of statistics; I wondered how I could enliven a bored and hungry crowd. Was this even possible?

Yes, I was in fine form, and knew I had the crowd interested and with me that morning. I called my speech "Bankers: Love'em or Hate'em" and showed two funny examples of a banker's decision, resulting in some loving the decision and others hating the banker for the same decision. I ended with these words, "A speech is like a love affair; it's easy to start one and hard to end it. So I will just say, thank you. Now, go eat!" I sat down to a standing ovation.

* * *

As I sipped on the last of my drink, I remembered being seated next to the Director of Public Relations for the American Bankers Association at the VIP luncheon. He had been invited to observe and assess the success of the program. We had a very lively conversation, and I learned a little about the ABA and he learned a lot about me. Over cocktails that evening we continued our getting-to-know-you session. After that, I was often asked to go whenever the ABA was asked to send a representative or a speaker to some function. I smiled as I came back to the present and thought about the speech I would soon be making.

Well Received

Jon Paul Brandt, Vice President of Public Relations at HSPC Bank met me at the airport and explained he had arranged for dinner at the Raffles Hotel with the reporter, James Beacon. Since Mr. Brandt was scheduled to be the Master of Ceremony at the luncheon the next day, he would attend the interview, with my permission. He hoped to pick up some pointers to use in my introduction. The interview was recorded and both the reporter and the MC took pages of notes. J. P. said he believed the Asiatic guests would like the same closing I had used at the California Bank session.

At lunch the next day, I met other VIPs of the Asian banking profession and learned that most spoke English. There would, however, be an interpreter for the large Chinese group in attendance. I also learned, to my consternation, that I was the first woman to attend the meeting of the ACU, and was the source of much wonderment and speculation.

Just before I was to give my speech, the MC waxed eloquently about my credentials, including my listing in the Who's Who. In the listing of "A Thousand Women of the World," I was right alongside Queen Elizabeth and Madam Curie. He ended by marveling at the opportunity America offered a person, "even a woman," to go from being a farmer's daughter in a small community to here, a speaker to the top international bankers.

After the applause quieted, I stood to begin my speech. All the Asiatic gentlemen in the room stood, which did not surprise me because I had noted before that Asiatic men out of respect stood when a woman entered a room or stood. We all sat down but I stood again to get eye contact with my listeners.

With puzzled expressions, and looking at each other for direction, they began to rise one by one, with much scraping of chairs, until all the men were standing. Oh my! What would I do? I sat down again, and asked the MC to tell the men that I, a woman, would not be offended if they sat while I stood.

Speaking in Mandarin, the language of business in Asia, he said something that made the men chuckle, and they remained seated when I next stood.

I explained the organization, function, and relationship of the American Bankers Association to the World Bank. It was rather dull stuff, and I must admit I was rather disconcerted by the interpreter. Following the advice of the MC, I ended with these words, "A speech is like a love affair. It's easy to start one, but very difficult to end it. So, I must say, thank you for listening." I sat down to a standing ovation.

* * *

After going to my room to pack, I decided to explore the Raffles Hotel, probably one of the most famous hotels in the world, and a remnant of the British colonial empire. That afternoon, John Paul and I toured Singapore, the cleanest, most memorable area of Asia. There was much to admire, from the young men in their crisp shorts standing on a pedestal in the middle of the intersection directing traffic, to the beautiful garden hiding tons and tons of garbage.

Later that evening as my plane took off for the twenty-two hour flight to California, I concluded that I had another interesting story to add to my treasure trove of events of a pioneer woman in a man's world of finance.

CHAPTER 29

Webster defines retirement *as a process of determining when to stop working at some scheduled job, say 9 to 5, usually for a wage or salary.*

We, the members of Nana's family, have always said she didn't know the meaning of the word retirement. *We believe you will agree with us when we tell you that as I am writing this on September 20, 2013, she is at the bank closing the purchase of a duplex complex. Even more remarkable is the fact that she is over ninety years old, and two years ago on her birthday she fell and did permanent damage to her hearing and eyesight. The doctor who treated her for the broken hip in the emergency room said she would never walk again. He didn't know my grandmother.*

Retirement: Full, Partial, or Not to Be?

Retirement is an ever-changing action that takes many different forms.

For example, my father officially retired three times because he did not like being idle. After a few weeks of 'retirement,' he would find another job. He repeated this several times. My husband, Jim, took a leave of absence from the school district to devote time to his real estate business. Twenty years later, Dr. J. R. Belt was still listed as an administrative staff member on-leave. He never did retire.

When I finally decided to retire officially and go on pension, I was rehired by the school president so my credentials could be counted. Some wealthy alumni had funded the President's Honors Program for five years. The top two students from each high school in California would be given room and board on campus, in addition to scholarships. But to induce these top students to enroll at CSU, all departments had to be certified by the national associations.

The School of Business was in danger of being de-certified. It was expanding exponentially, and the administration had been forced to hire many young teachers whose doctorates were a-work-in-process and did not count for accreditation. My credentials and other honors went a long way to balance the score.

Before 1983, Jim and I had tentatively discussed the pros and cons of retiring. He had already begun the slow process of retirement, devoting less and less time to hands-on management of GEM Realty and more time to mega deals. Using creative financing such as trusts, partnerships, insurance, and non-profits, he was able to involve us financially in those deals. I had been on the CSU staff for twenty years, and had stopped doing so much off-campus activity, feeling I had already established my place in what had formerly been a man's world of finance.

While considering retirement, two vital decisions are when and where.

In my case, the *when* was influenced by California's offer of early retirement to professors with at least twenty years of employment. The aim was to save money and probably to get rid of the old codgers and replace them with younger, more liberal professors. The unexpected result was a shortage of highly qualified profs in the School of Business and a threat of decertification.

The window of opportunity to take early retirement in exchange for a five-year advance on the pension scale ended in September, 1983. So it was time for me to retire.

When I announced my intention to retire in January, 1983, I was offered a lucrative five-year post-retirement contract to teach one class for one semester each year. When I signed, I realized that part of the *where* decision had been made. We had been watching the development of a senior community about five miles from the campus. In addition to the latest state-of-the-art, two bedroom, two bath homes with the current architectural craze of a great room, there was a clubhouse with every amenity. We decided to downsize to a 2100 sq. ft. trouble free house and put our 7000 sq. ft. home up for sale. A Saudi bought it for cash, and because any deposit over $10,000 had to be reported to the government, we spent the better part of the next year filtering smaller amounts of cash into the banking system.

I recalled some of the words in a popular song "Come to California to work, but go to Florida to retire." That seemed to be the prevailing advice of the day, so we decided to take a second look at a number of brochures that had come into the realty office via MLS. One that appealed to us described a project being developed on Estero Island off the western coast of Florida and about fifty miles west of Fort Meyers. It was semi-tropical with cooling breezes creating a pleasant year round temperature. One main cobblestone road bisected the island, running from the northern most tip to the southernmost tip, allowing for ocean front condo hi-rises on both sides of the road.

We selected a condo that faced the coast and only blocks from the inter-island ferry's docks. It was a 2/2 with a large dorm to provide "bunk space for the hordes of friends who will want to visit you in your tropical island haven." That part had limited appeal to us, but it was nice to have if needed. The units were fully furnished with a choice of color scheme: blue-green, red-pink, orange-brown or white-black. We chose the blue-green cool color scheme.

The unique thing about this development was that each unit had its own dock with a small power boat that could be rented for $1.00 per month. Wow!

There were two deciding factors for us. The first was the development company had a very active worldwide rental division that promised a 10% investment return when the owner was "in absentia." The second factor was private cars were not allowed on the island. Colorful two decker buses provided free transportation for residents. For those of us from Southern California, or elsewhere, who have suffered years of bumper-to-bumper traffic the absence of cars seemed like heaven-on-earth. All we had to say was, "Sign me up!"

Then, as if by design to create a perfect retirement plan, a couple came into a GEM office in Orange County. They wanted to trade a small farm in Oregon for property in O.C. so they could be near their grandchildren. They had pictures showing a well maintained three bedroom house and a large barn.

The foot print of the three-acre farm showed it to be a cleared, mostly level plot with a stream and small pond. Jim showed them some property we had acquired in a trade and they chose one. After Jim, who is in my opinion the world's best horse trader, finished negotiating, we ended up with a three-acre farm *and* a three bedroom house, sparsely furnished, *and* a big red barn with two riding horses, *and* a small tractor with cultivating attachments.

Now everything was in place for an early retirement. Our daughter and her husband hosted a retirement party for us in their grand Huntington Harbour home. The *time* was set for January 1983 and the *where* promised variety and entertainment. From January to June, we would be on our Florida island home fishing, boating, writing, and reading. Then it would be off to Oregon, where we and the grandchildren could enjoy a healthy summer on the farm and away from the smoggy, crowded city. September would find us back home in California for work and school. I had chosen to fulfill my post retirement contract in the fall semester. That allowed us to be home at The Quad for Thanksgiving and Christmas Holidays. It also allowed me to continue to serve as a judge for the HH Boat Parade, which was my major social event of the year.

But as Wee Robby Burns said, "The best made plans of mice and men often go astray." When one makes plans that involve others, things can and most often do go off track.

CHAPTER 30

When Nana mentioned that she was bored stiff at the afternoon teas spon-
sored by the management of the 'Pelican Nest,' the high rise on the island, I
could understand. She always said she had a hard time talking to women.
And I laughed when she said the men who might talk her language only
wanted to talk about fishing. Thus she cut her retirement on the island short.

Retirement: On the Island

Our best made plans began to go wrong. Jim announced that he could
not leave for Florida as planned, on January 10th, because one of his
mega deals did not close on time. However, he insisted I go on, and he
would join me as soon as possible. That was fine with me because the
quiet and solitude would allow me to work on the book (no title yet)
I wanted to write.

When around friends and relatives and things to be done, the book took
second place. For example, the first two weeks of our official retirement
were spent moving from our 7000 sq. ft. home to the Quad, the name
given to this community of small homes near the university. We had to
cherry-pick enough to furnish two bedrooms and the great room, which
was all the rage at that time. It was four rooms in one.

Entering the front door to a small living room, usually the biggest waste
of space in a traditional house, we furnished it with lightweight chairs
that could be moved into the next space, which was designed as a TV,
rec, or office room. This multipurpose room got the most use. We put in

a game table, and often ate there rather than in the formal dining room in the next space. Even with leaves taken out of our dining room table so that it seated only six, we found it too crowded. The kitchen, with all its gleaming appliances, would have pleased the most demanding cooks, which I am not, completed the great room. Did I say retirement? I had never worked so hard, or maybe it was old age.

Choosing what to take and what to leave for the Arab buyers was exhausting. I had to make many trips between houses to measure furniture and to measure space to determine whether it would fit. I had to give up many pieces that I wanted because they were simply too big. When the 10th finally arrived, I was glad to fly (flee) to Florida and leave the rest to Jim.

My arrival in Florida was an anti-climax. The developer had written that I would be met at the Fort Meyers airport, then escorted to a private cruiser where an ample feast awaited as we sailed to my new home. I waited and waited some more until my two suitcases were the only ones going round and round on the carousel. I must do something!

I went in search for a porter and a taxi. My plan was to go to the interisland landing dock and take my chances that I would find my way to the Pelican Nest once I arrived at Estero Island. When I and my two very heavy suitcases were delivered to the dock, I heard my name being called over the public address system. When identified, a very hurried man of Mexican descent explained in very broken English that he was told to meet me at the dock. After looking again at my letter, which very clearly said that I would be met at the airport, I realized there was a problem of communication. I was somewhat mollified when the hostess met me in the elegant foyer of our condo complex and apologized profusely. After that it seemed management went out of their way to make me feel welcome, but there were many areas of miscommunication.

I spent the first two weeks exploring my environment: a new home, new furniture, and new boat. I took hundreds of photographs, so that I would have a picture inventory in case of a dispute over rental damages. Management sponsored a shopping trip to Fort Meyers, and I was glad to get some needed items I had not packed. Most of the long term residents bought food either to fix their own favorite dishes or to save money. I soon realized that food was an item we had not factored into our island retirement plans.

When I first arrived, I was delighted to find breakfast staples in the refrigerator: bacon, eggs, bread, juice, tea, and coffee, cereal and milk, lots of jams and jellies. But I was on my own when these were gone. There was a small convenience store and diner in our condo complex, as there was at every major development, but prices were at least twenty-five percent higher than the mainland. Almost every morning, a group of women rode the double decker bus up and down the island comparison shopping and occasionally finding a bargain. One woman said, "We live to eat, since we must eat to live."

What a paradox! Live on an expensive island, but spend your time hunting for affordable food.

When I grew tired of the so-so food at the condo diner, I boarded the double deck bus and went hunting for something different. I found a KFC, the ever present McDonald's, and several fine diners. I thought that when Jim arrived, we could dress up and go out each Friday until we have sampled each one. What a very weak ambition.

I took our boat out a few times, but never far from shore because I was not, and never would be, a sailor. I tried my hand at fishing, but when I did not get a bite from a fish but received several from some nasty insects, I gave up and went home after about twenty minutes. So much for one of the great activities on the island!

Heading Home

Now it was high time to settle down and work on my book (still untitled). But increasingly I found myself striving to remember a date or person, or even how to spell a particular place. The manuscript was full of blanks waiting for answers. (This was well before Google, the Internet, or even the PC.)

Computers were large, ponderous machines made by IBM and kept in temperature controlled rooms. The typewriter was the main instrument of written communication, and the written word found in libraries was a major source of information. I was making one or more trips to the P.M. library each week. I was often frustrated because I could not find the information I needed.

The library was adequate for its time and place, but could not compare favorably to the great libraries at universities in Southern California. So, to make the trip worthwhile, I would buy as many groceries as I could carry. The IGA store near the docks did a land-office business catering to residents of the off shore islands. I wondered if it would be possible or profitable to put a small version of a big chain, like Wal-Mart, on the island. Probably not, or Wal-Mart would already be there.

When Jim called in mid-February to say he might not be able to come to Florida at all this year, it crystallized my growing discontent with island living, and the high cost of everything bothered my Scottish soul. The bugs made going outside a challenge to be endured, and in the background was the fear of hurricanes. The reason I gave for my early departure was that I could not find the material I needed and could not work on my book. However the real reason was loneliness.

Management provided a high tea every afternoon, but most who attended were women, and I was never good at talking to my own gender, so I soon avoided it. I could not find anyone who spoke my language. The men, who might have talked about investing and business, talked about fishing and boating.

I decided to leave Florida as soon as possible. I authorized the developer to rent or sell our unit. I vowed to have the men at GEM realty push the sale, even at a loss, if necessary. With my bags checked in, I boarded a plane ready to fly (flee) back to Southern California and Jim at the Quad. Thus ended my misadventure of retirement on an island.

California here I come . . . again!

CHAPTER 31

My grandparents had difficulty understanding why I would prefer one week at the equestrian camp, when they could offer me the use of a horse all summer long. They didn't know because I hadn't told them, but I got my first kiss from a boy behind the livery stables and I was hoping he would come back for the coming summer; unfortunately he didn't.

Retirement: at the Farm

A glance at the calendar on the kitchen wall of our home at the Quad made me realize that Jim and I should be amassing and packing items that will be needed to implement the second phase of our retirement plan. We had devised an ambitious plan that involved three locations with varied activities and multiple interests. Ah, but once again the words of wee Bobby Burns would hold true.

I hoped the second phase of our retirement would go more according to plan than the first, but somehow I doubted it. Our main reason for acquiring the farm was to provide a place away from the crowded city where we and the grandchildren could spend a quiet, hassle free summer. We quickly learned that it is best to ask the recipient *if* that is what they consider best. To a man, or a girl, in this case, they considered it a punishment—spend an entire summer on a farm, in the middle of nowhere, with grandparents as their only playmates?

They all said, "Although we love you dearly, you know what we mean."

They preferred the noisy city with friends, and although the farm had two rented horses, our grandchildren had been sooo looking forward to the two weeks at the equestrian camp to meet their friends again. Thus,we old folks would spend a quiet, restful summer without the rambunctiousness of grandchildren.

A Lost Cause

With a small U-Haul trailing behind our van, as we crossed the border into Oregon, it began to rain. I was reminded of a friend who once said "In Oregon, you don't dare leave home without an umbrella."

The weather cleared up in a couple of days, and we were able to get out and survey our 3.5 acre kingdom. The sellers had started a vegetable garden and labeled the rows, Kale, Kumquats, and Brussels, which were foreign to me; but some I knew, like peas, corn, and tomatoes. They all looked green and healthy. There were weeds, or were those the kale plants? They also looked green and healthy. Jim was proud of the little tractor with its six attachments, all designed to help the gentleman-farmer.

Then there was the mud. The soil in our part of Oregon was a clay-like substance which, when wet, stuck to everything—shoes, clothes, and tools—and when it dried, it was like cement. It rained nearly every day. Within a week I had given up my garden to the weeds. Jim's tractor with its shiny attachments soon became clogged with mud. If we had a clear day, he would be trying to wash the mud off, which was quite a chore.

During the latter part of the fall, I quickly learned that everyone became involved in canning peaches. One Wednesday, a delegation of Farmets (farmer's wives) invited me to join them on the following Friday. I was advised to bring a bushel of peaches and I could can enough to last all year.

Since I wanted to belong, I was happy to join them. I showed up bright and early with my bushel of peaches but the day went downhill from then on. I didn't have knives or Mason jars; what the heck were Mason jars?

Finally, with borrowed equipment from the "Farmets," I started to peel peaches. Before long, the juice was running off my elbows and ruining the cutsie dress I had bought because it looked like what I thought a farm wife would wear, like Daisy-Mae. Wrong again! These Farmets looked sharp. I finally went home, almost in tears, with three Mason jars, borrowed, of badly mangled peaches. My PhD degree had not taught me a thing about canning peaches. Talk about a fish out of water!

Sleeping was another adventure. The sellers had left the house sparsely but basically furnished. We were as delighted as children when we discovered the big feather mattress in the master bedroom. It was a gem and more comfortable than our Tempur-pedic. We wondered why they weren't sold in bulk, and speculated on a possible way to capitalize on them. But we soon found a flaw in our gem.

A restless sleeper would cause the feathers to move until he/she was sleeping on a featherless bed, with only two thin sheets between themselves and the bed springs. After a particularly trying and exhausting rainy day, we awakened that night to a strange sight—a mountain of feathers between us. We were both sleeping on the bed springs. We looked at each other across the feathers and I wondered who would admit defeat first. Then I yelled, "Let's go home!"

"Amen," said Jim, and he jumped into the mountain of feathers and I followed. We laughed and played, glad that a decision had been made.

During the week, Jim contacted a Realtor and listed the house for sale while I packed. There was not much to pack since we left all the mud-caked shoes, clothes, and my cutsie dress in the waste bin. Once again it was, "California, here we come!"

CHAPTER 32

California became like a magnet drawing my grandparents back from wherever—an island in Florida, a farm in Oregon, or any other place they thought of as a retirement haven. California thus became the ultimate retirement spot. And I was as happy as they were to see them come home!

Retirement: Back Home

Jim and I traveled in silence as we drove south on I-5, crossed the border between Oregon and California, then down the long length of the state.

We were thinking of things that must be done as a result of our abrupt change in plans. Jim was probably thinking of alternative plans for the disposal of the farm in case the local Realtor was not successful in selling it. He told me later that he was also contemplating his reception at the office. He had been subjected to teasing by employees, who could not picture him as a farmer.

What will Joe say? Jim had made him the boss while he was away, and a proud Joe had the promise of a stellar summer.

I had to prioritize the many things I had done to close one house for three months and open another. Now everything had to be reversed. I must stop the forwarding of mail, but must get the electricity restored first. Unless we stopped overnight somewhere on the way south, we would arrive home after midnight. Where were the flashlights or the candles stashed? What about the matches? Round and round our thoughts traveled as we mentally tried to get the Quad ready for occupancy once again.

A Fortunate Turn

A couple of days after our homecoming, I decided to visit my office at CSU, and what a fortunate decision that was! As a part of my post-retirement contract with CSU I had asked to retain my office of twenty some years. Over time, I had made it uniquely mine with plants, pictures, and one entire wall of framed letters, depicting honors, commendations, and scenes of triumph. I called this my ego wall.

The demand for office space had been satisfied with the opening of the huge seven-story School of Business building across campus. On my desk was a note asking me to call as soon as possible. I learned that President Wade of Brigham Young University (BYU of Hawaii) had visited the campus looking for me, and was disappointed when told I was gone for the summer, but left a number to call just in case. When I reached Dr. Wade, I learned he had booked a flight to Hawaii the next day, but would interrupt it to meet with me on campus instead.

We met in the new faculty dining room and I learned that he wanted to establish a new division of international studies and international finance would be an important part of the studies. A Jewish Rabbi had urged him to contact me. After discussing terms and conditions, I decided to accept the challange of creating something out of nothing.

During the next month I learned more about BYU. It had a fixed student body of 2000, and was established by the Mormons for the purpose of providing an education for youth from the Polynesian Islands. The quality of high school graduates varied widely. Often a student was recruited for his or her skill in their island's special art form—singing, dancing, weaving, or flaming sword play—but was barely out of the jungle with regard to higher education. I searched the libraries for suitable texts and supporting reading material for such a varied group.

In mid-July I was met at the Honolulu airport by the administrative assistant, Dr. Margarietta Waii, ("Just call me Marge Why") and was escorted to the President's house, which was to be my home for the next two weeks.

Marge was such an entertaining and fun loving person, and I was in a happy and receptive mood when I met Mrs. Wade and five of her seven children. I still remember with pleasure, the happiness and love I found in that home.

I spent a lot of time with the librarians, outlining the course work for the semester with its suggested reading material. We ordered books and designated a special shelf for students of international finance. We ordered newspapers with special emphasis on finance, including The Wall Street Journal and Barrons. Although I worked diligently on my assignment, I got in more than my fair share of entertainment.

One morning, by prearrangement, Jay Fox, the director of the fabulous Pacific Island Revue, invited me to spend the day with him. We started by boating down the man-made river that flowed between the villages. Each island had a designated section of land on which they constructed a village that resembled one on their own island. As our boat came into view, each village put on a show best representing the skill of their homeland. We docked at each one for fifteen to twenty minutes.

We reached the Hawaiian village at noontime. We disembarked and enjoyed a typical Hawaiian Luau, complete with a roasted pig. I was told they had plans to offer this typical luau to visiting tourists for $5.00. If the visitors received half of what I got, it would be a bargain.

We boarded our boat again and continued visiting other villages where the women exhibited their handicraft. There were woven shawls, baskets, and ropes galore, with plans to sell these items to tourists. One brown-eyed maiden from Timor explained this would give the women from her village another outlet for their woven goods. Bravo! The students were learning the economic laws of supply and demand.

After a tasty repast at a New Zealand village, we hurried to the huge stage to see the noted, or must see production of "The Pacific Islands Revue."

I was escorted to the director's box. He said he might join me if there were not too many problems backstage.

While I waited for the show to begin, I remembered that Mr. Fox had told me he would be gone for the month of August, interviewing candidates for the show who were also student material. He was authorized to offer them room and board if they worked in the Revue, which was a big money maker for BYU because every tour of the Island included a visit to the Revue at $25.00 per head.

All too soon, my two weeks was over and I headed home. During the month of August, I lazed around the pool or ocean, did some research at well known libraries, and generally waited for the semester to begin so that I could get back to work. Retirement does not resonate well with me! Finally, September arrived.

Lasting Changes

When the fall semester began, I taught the required one, three-hour class in Investment Analysis. I also volunteered for a second, and would have taken on a third if they would have let me. After all, I was drawing retirement pay and one semester's salary.

The Christmas season was drawing near. Jim and I had planned a round of parties, days with our grandchildren, and I agreed again to join a three-man panel to judge the boats in the Hunting Harbour Boat Parade. How things had changed from their humble beginnings, when the homeowners decorated their own boats. Now professionals were hired. We increased the number of categories of winners. After all, when a man pays thousands of dollars, he expects to win a silver cup.

In moments of quiet respite, we realized that we had to make a decision. The condo and boat on Estero Island west of Florida sat empty and waiting for us. Jim was reluctant to leave the office for five months, and I didn't look forward to spending five months all alone with no activity. But what about our condo?

Then, like a bolt of lightning, another option came via a call from President Wade at BYU in Hawaii. He wondered if I would come to Hawaii and teach classes in international finance to the teachers who would be teaching it next semester. He offered room and board and transportation.

Could I come in about two weeks for the start of the spring semester? I would and I could! Jim would be happy because he could stay home and work at his own pleasure at his GEM office. I would be happy working among people I had learned to love. We put the Florida condo up for immediate sale at terms that made it easy to sell. The relief we both felt when we learned that we didn't have to go was a deciding factor.

New Adventures

Trading one island for another energized me. I called Marge Why and told her I was ready to come. She said the VIP house on campus was being redecorated for me and almost ready. We agreed on a time of arrival and she agreed to meet me again.

My semester at BYU lived up to my lofty expectations. There were so many memorable experiences. For example, the two bedroom VIP house had been the home for the President, but when Dr. Wade was appointed as President, a much bigger house off campus had to be found for him. The house on campus stood empty for many years until Mrs. Wade decided to make it a VIP house and oversaw the remodeling. I happened to be its first occupant.

Often during my tenancy, a student would ask to see the finished product and announce proudly they had worked on the remodeling. Also my presence on campus made me very aware of the 7 to 10 o'clock study period.

At 10 p.m. the quiet campus became a noisy beehive of activity with singing and dancing for an hour until lights out, when the campus became quiet again.

Most of the students led a sort of dual life. It was strange to see a student struggling with the concept of the World Bank by day, and recognize him by night as the native wearing a loin cloth, climbing a coconut tree. I was touched when students, knowing that I was not a Mormon, came on Saturday night with a meat dish or a piece of fruit so that I would not be hungry on "Fast Sunday" when everything was closed, including McDonald's off campus.

There were many Chinese at BYU, and one of them asked me if there was any way I could help her get to California. When I mentioned this to President Wade, he asked me not to offer encouragement. He said the reason China sent so many of their top students to BYU was because we sent them back to China after graduation.

All too soon the semester ended and I, too, had to go back home. After days and even weeks, visiting family and friends, I settled down to seriously work on my planned book. The farm was sold, and thus ended that part of our grandiose retirement plan.

Back into Routine

The fall semester started, and the pages the book I had started writing continued to fly out of my typewriter to the editor's ghostwriter. The Christmas season came and went, and we were again faced with the necessity to decide whether to go to our Florida island condo when two things happened. First, we received an offer from a buyer for our condo, and another call came from President Wade. Would I accept the honor of being asked to deliver the graduation address and could I come for a week in May to enjoy the many activities? I would and I could.

The last two years of my post-retirement contract were spent at home.

My book on the relatively complicated theory of investment analysis found a moderate success among a limited group of scholars. (After all, the goal is to get published, not to make money.) My tenure at CSU was about to come to an end.

CHAPTER 33

As my Nana was finishing this chapter and bringing her life story to an end, I was looking through the boxes of tapes and found several interesting titles we weren't able to cover. For example: A Fulbright at the National University of Chili; On loading the Mercedes at Amsterdam; Incident on the border between Hong Kong and Communist China; Touring the world on one small island—New Zealand; and Searching for ice cubes in England. Next I found a folder marked A French Connection with five shorter chapters in it.

There are many more items in other boxes. Maybe someday I'll write another biography or series of short stories.

The End? Or is it?

An autobiography, by its definition, must come to an end. With that inevitability, the question then becomes *when*? I could have ended my story when I was listed in "Who's Who in America" because I had reached my goal as first stated when I was in the 5th grade. I could have ended it when I reached my goal of being the first woman appointed to an all-male staff in the School of Business at a major university. Or I might have ended my story when we reached California after trying for twenty years.

After World War II, we planned to join the exodus to California, the land of golden opportunity, but something always interfered: a job that was too good to pass up, a doctoral scholarship, a sabbatical. A more logical time would be when I retired from CSU. However, I am eighty-eight-years-old as I write these words, and there is a lot of living to be done, and a lot of economic history to be recorded.

My life seemed to be divided into twenty-year segments, 1923, my birth date; 1943, my marriage and a BS degree; 1963, my arrival in California; 1983, my retirement. Many things that happened during these segments helped shape my future and helped me succeed as a woman in a man's world of business and finance. 1923 to 1945 were the years of the Great Depression, Roosevelt's Bank Holiday (when I lost my $28), and the discovery of oil, which ended the depression for the McKemmie clan, my winning the Illinois Best Speaker's contest, graduating with top honors, going to SIU on a resulting scholarship, and meeting the handsome cadet who was to be my husband for fifty-three years. 1943 to 1963 were the years of World War II and its resulting shortages of civilian goods, of the post war prosperity, of my marriage, of working for the Navy, of the birth of our daughter, of teaching art, economics, algebra and dramatics, of being named "Illinois Best Teacher" by the Ford Foundation. Using the very generous award funds, I was able to get a PhD degree.

I was often asked how much *luck* played in my career. If luck is defined as opportunity meeting preparation, then yes, luck played a big part. I tried to learn by reading, reading, and more reading! On an evaluation a student once wrote, "She knows more about more things than anyone on campus, but if you want an 'A' run like hell!" Being prepared also means being known. I volunteered for pro bono work, because someone in the audience might see an opportunity and remember me for it. I was lucky I had a family, especially my husband who was so cooperative. He was not like that businessman, who said, "If you were my wife, you would be at home, where you belong, having babies." Another lucky factor was my uniqueness; there were not many women in the world of finance. If there were several women instead of just one in that Federal Reserve picture, Ralph Edwards would have never featured my story on his program "This is Your Life."

When the government started the "Equal Opportunity Program" for minorities, which included women, banks and other financial organizations were scrambling to find qualified women so they could be politically correct.

Had I not spoken before so many bankers who were Elks, Rotarians, or Lions, I would not have been remembered and recommended for the Union Bank Board of Directors. Had I not made that speech as a bank director, I would not have met the PR man from the American Bankers Association. I am glad that I did my part to make it easier for the women who followed me, but for me it's over.

A Different View

It would be very different if I were to try to break into the field today.

My competition would include hoards of competent women from all over the world with multiple degrees. Enrollment in schools of business has tipped the scale in favor of women. Even the much desired MBA Programs at eastern universities are being invaded in increasing numbers by women graduates.

More power to them!

An autobiography, like a love affair, is easy to begin, but difficult to end so I will simply say: "Thank you for reading my story."

CHAPTER 34

A Will in Focus

The Benevolent Matriarch

Wow, *matriarch*—my biggest challenge and the one dearest to my heart. After all, what do we work for? The life stories collected and described were a backdrop for the family I love. The life experiences and the love I've received from my beloved father and mother as well as all of my extended family has been the highlight of my life.

I look at my life as one would at a patchwork quilt, drawing from stories experienced and passed down. While my husband and I raised our daughter, we enjoyed sharing these family memories.

Patricia also had a calling to teach. She is her own person, but in that way followed in our footsteps. I tried, through example, to instill a sense of confidence in my family. Having a daughter and two granddaughters, I especially wanted to teach these women, who were temporarily under my watch, that with the right mindset you can accomplish the righteous desires of your heart . . . and mind. Even when your dreams do not quite fit the mold.

Each of my granddaughters is also raising a son. It has been shown down through the ages that the influence of the mother is paramount in shaping a strong man. Teaching him courage, self-discipline, and a strong foundation for life, tempered with a loving and charitable spirit are the hallmarks of a great mother. I am proud to say they are both well equipped to accomplish this.

As I contemplate my family, I ask myself what new adventures lay ahead. But I also look back with a sense of awe. My life looks like a picture, broken down as a puzzle, interlocking and connecting the different pieces. It's amazing how, with all the different challenges, curves, and forks in the road, the picture has been completed to a certain degree of perfection. Each time I made a conscious choice it led me to the next path.

We ask ourselves, "What if?" Well, it all comes down to choices.

Certainly we are influenced by those around us and our environment, especially when we are young and naive. However, from our earliest memory and beyond we have our own natural instincts that guide and direct us, and even then we were making choices. Each time we meet another force, it builds us up like an architect commanding a design. To quote Tennyson, "One equal temper of heroic hearts made weak by time and fate, but strong in will to strive, to seek, to find and not to yield."

As I enter into my 90s, my life continues to be an unfolding adventure. I have a deep personal relationship with my Lord God. We converse often. When I start a speech or new project I say, "Please help me."

Or when I avoid some danger or bad decision I say, "Thank You." I often go to sleep reciting refrains from a favorite song, *What a friend I have in Jesus.*

"Can we find a friend so faithful who will all our sorrows share, Jesus knows our every weakness, take it to the Lord in prayer."

POSTSCRIPT 1

Matriarch Queen

My Nana's life has been an incredible one! She's been an inspiration to all who have known her, whether stranger or friend or family member.

When I think of my Nana I think of the words Matriarch Queen. As a sun kissed, freckled face child of eight, I would sit in her grand study behind her large mahogany desk, on two stacks of yellow pages, and pretend to rule the world! (I often thought that this was Nana's job.) I would type reports with the speed of lightening without looking at the keys. I checked the market and bought and sold my stocks. I prepared deeds, filed foreclosures, took imaginary meetings and advised big businesses like Mattel, McDonald's, and Chuck E. Cheese on how to improve their businesses and increase their stock portfolios.

In my world, Nana was always The Boss. Wherever life took us she was the head; she was treated like royalty, highly respected, sought after, and often feared. She was kind and compassionate, strong willed, sharp and stern.

If you needed to knock down an obstacle, right a wrong, or figure out an unconventional way to solve a problem, everyone (family, friends and colleagues) would break out the big guns and enlist Nana's help. She was the busiest person anyone ever knew, yet she continued to take on and conquer new projects all the time.

On my vacation days from school, I would often accompany her on her daily conquests. My favorite part was bank row. We would visit multiple banks handling much business, all the while filling my tummy with complimentary tea and cookies. (I had once recommended that we do all of our business with the bank that had the best selection of tantalizing treats.)

After our big business day was over, Nana would switch from Dr. Belt, first lady of finance, into my mere grandmother. We would make homemade caramel apples, build tents, play cards, throw tea parties, and plan future excursions in the motor home appropriately named Mimi after me.

My experience and perception of being born a woman was vastly different than that of my Nana's. I was extremely aware of the respect, importance, and power that my grandmother held and wielded. What I did not realize was she had accomplished this despite being a woman. She taught me through word and example to be strong and to believe in myself; to never take "no" for an answer; to be tenacious, creative, and unconventional; to persevere and to believe that with enough effort and drive, anything is possible. Because of her I have always been proud to be a woman.

POSTSCRIPT 2

Warm Memories

Verses from a card given to my Nana on her 90th birthday:

"Bring on the birthdays! Each decade represents a new chapter of living and learning . . .

Every new milestone's a moment to enjoy with rich friendship, spontaneous laughter, and warm memories.

The life you've lived has been truly amazing. And today, as you look back on nine happy decades, remember how much you've accomplished and how much you're admired.

HAPPY 90th!"

Love,
Melinda

Dr. Belt explaining The Wall Street Journal articles to her class at
USC in 1970.

The capable biographer, Michele (Mimi) Wager,
granddaughter of the author working on Dr. Belt's memoirs
2011-2013.

Michele at work: teaching a new dance step.

Dr. J. R. Belt and Dr. Virginia Belt on their 50th wedding anniversary, June 6, 1993.

The author and granddaughter, Melinda L. McGill, on their way to an enhancement meeting where Dr. Belt was the scheduled speaker in 2008.

Dr. Belt and daughter, Patricia L. McGill, at the bottom of the
grand staircase on the Love Boat in 2009.

As the years go by...

3 years

Scout - 11 years

High School Grad - 17 Years

College Grad - 19 years

File Photo - 33 Years

Honors - 53 years

The Farmer's Daughter - 84 years

Formal Tea - 88 years